The Celts of Ancient Gaul (France)

David B. McCoy

I would like to thank my proofreaders Mary Ann D'Aurelio and Dr. Rhonda Baughman.

Cover image from Creative Commons.

Today, the Gallic rooster (*con qaulois*) is an unofficial national symbol of France. During the time of Ancient Rome, historian Suetonius, in *The Twelve Caesars*, noticed that, in Latin, rooster (gallus) and Gauls (Gallus) were homonyms (words which sound alike or are spelled alike, but have different meaning. Contrary to *Marianne*, who embodies France as a republic, the Gallic rooster represents France as a nation.

Spare Change Press®
Massillon, OH 44646
sparechangepress79@gmail.com

Preface

Adapted from Top 10 Fascinating Facts About the Celts

A *TopTenz* Video on YouTube

Historians have concluded the Celts didn't originate in Ireland – or Scotland, or Wales, or even England, for that matter. Instead, their roots have been traced back to central Europe.

Emerging from the late Bronze Age along the Danube River, Celtic tribes are believed to have initially lived throughout continental Europe. Eventually, these tribes expanded north and did settle in the United Kingdom. But when you think of ancient tribal warriors from Ireland, the odds are you're not thinking of the Celts; you're [actually] thinking of the Gaels (a Gaelic-speaking Celt in Ireland or Scotland or the Isle of Man).

The group you think of as the "Celts" isn't really the Celts, at least not in the sense that the Romans were the Romans, or the Greeks were the Greeks. That's because the Celts weren't just one group; they consisted of many, including the previously mentioned Gaels, the Britons, the Gauls (of France), and the Galatians, among others. [You] see, "Celtic" really referred to language, and the somewhat similar dialects these various tribes used.

Some historians suggest the languages were different enough, and the groups so spread out (as far east as Turkey, all the way west to the Atlantic Ocean) that it's highly unlikely most of the tribes were remotely united. In fact, it's believed part of the reason they were ultimately defeated by the Romans was because of their lack of unification.

Introduction

We don't know precisely where Celts came from, nor how they integrated with the indigenous cultures they encountered. There appears to be no clear or continuous archeological record of Celtic migration or occupation, and little consensus between scholars concerning Celtic genetics and language. However, from 1000 BCE onwards, the wide-ranging Celts introduced their Indo-European language to a wide variety of peoples throughout the continent. As a result, the Celtic tongue was understood, if not adopted, as a common language of convenience (*lingua franca*) — much like the English language is today.

The Celts were the first European people north of the Alps to emerge into recorded history. But the Celts did not leave any extensive written testimony in their own language. Celtic history, philosophy, religion, and law were transmitted orally. This was not because the Celts were illiterate but because of a religious prohibition. Julius Cesar noted that druids thought it unlawful to commit this knowledge to writing for two reasons. First, they did not want the details of their culture to become common knowledge. Second, they thought those who relied on writing were less likely to cultivate their memory. Thus, in trying to understand Celtic motivations, attitudes, philosophies, and laws, we find ourselves handicapped.

It was not until the Greeks and Romans began to write their accounts of the Celts that they emerged into recorded history. However, these accounts were sometimes culturally flawed and invariably biased. The Greeks and Romans depicted the Celts as barbaric, fierce warriors, proud, illiterate, given to childish amusements, and often drunk. In other words, Rome and Greece represented 'civilization' while the Celts were exotic barbarians.

Caesar, himself, has led to some historical confusion by referring to the Celts of what is today France, as Gauls. Adding to this, academics have divided the Celts into two main groups. Continental Celts are the Celtic-speaking people of mainland Europe, and Insular Celts are the Celtic-speaking peoples of the British and Irish islands and their descendants. Thus, Gauls are Continental Celts. One problem which arises in studying the Celts is that authors tend to move back and forth between the Continental and Insular Celts without specifically letting the reader know which group they are writing about.

At about the same time Caesar was invading Gaul, another movement was slowly gaining hold in the world: Christianity. This new religion, which taught there is only one God instead of many, began spreading through Europe during the first century CE. By the fourth century, there were Christian communities in many areas of Gaul.

As Christianity spread, many members of the Gallic ruling and intellectual classes embraced this new faith. And as it grew in power, religious leaders in Gaul put pressure on local groups to give up their pagan faith in the old gods. To encourage this, temples were destroyed and churches were built in their place. Writings and artworks that depicted the pagan gods were deliberately destroyed. Anyone who worshipped Celtic gods were stripped of their civil rights.

Things were somewhat different in Britain and Ireland. Rome had little influence on daily life, so people continued to worship the Celtic gods and follow their traditional ways of life. It is unknown exactly when Christianity arrived in Ireland and Britain, but by the fifth century CE, it was firmly established.

As in Gaul, many Celtic kings of the British Isles converted to Christianity, and so did their tribes. As luck would have it, many former druids embraced Christianity, and as a result, the Christian church over time allowed for the recording of Celtic mythology, heroes, gods, and legends. They also were permitted to decorate the pages of their manuscripts and bibles with extraordinary artwork in the style of the great swirling forms and designs of the La Tène period (described in chapter two). Also, Celtic art flourished under Christianity, where carvers creating magnificent stone crosses adorned with Celtic swirls and knotwork.

Despite the recording of various aspects of Celtic culture by the druids and monks, it was not until the 16th and 17th centuries CE that scholars established a link between the Celtic languages of old and more modern forms of these languages of Ireland and the United Kingdom. At the time, the Welshman Edward Lhuyd and the Scotsman George Buchanan used classical sources to prove the Gaelic languages of Ireland, Wales, Brittany, and Scotland had a common Celtic root. Until then, the term Celt had been applied only to Celtic people on the European continent.

In spite of scholarly efforts in the 1700s, the word "Celt" did not come into widespread use until the romantic movement of the 18th century, triggered by an outbreak of "Celtomania." Celtomania was a variety of movements and trends that saw a renewed interest in aspects of an idealized Celtic culture. Artists and writers of this mania drew on the traditions of Gaelic literature and so-called "Celtic" or "Insular" art. As a result of both the Church's inclusion of some of the Celtic traditions, and Celtomania, the term "Celtic" became associated with the British Isles, as noted in the Preface.

As previously noted, in trying to write about the Celts, one faces a major hurdle—the Celts left no written records. Consequently, we are left with three main classes of evidence regarding the ancient Celts: documentary, linguistic, and archaeological. Each gives us a range of complementary information with which to create a picture of Celtic societies.

Documentary sources: These comprise all the written material related to the Celts, from texts on coins to stone inscriptions, and recorded histories by Greeks, Romans, Christians and druids. Textual analysis has many drawbacks as well as advantages. We are limited by what remains. There are many things we would like to know about the past, but if no one chose to write them down, or if texts were lost, we are out of luck. We are also at the mercy of the biases of those who wrote the texts that do survive. These authors were not necessarily trying to enlighten us on the points about which we have questions. In some cases, authors were distorting the past for their own purposes.

Linguistics: Another discipline essential to understanding the Celts is historical linguistics, the study of how languages are related to each other and how they change over time. Languages can be related to each other almost the way family members are related to each other, or like branches of a tree. Historical linguists try to determine how closely related to each other different languages are, and this can allow them to make certain hypotheses about the people who spoke them. Through historical linguistics we can deduce important facts about social practices, beliefs, and identity.

Archaeological evidence: Archaeology is the study of the human past using material remains. These remains can be any objects that people created, modified, or used. Archaeologists want to know what these people's daily lives were like, how they were governed, how they interacted with each other, and what they believed and valued. Archaeology is based on the scientific method. They ask questions and develop hypotheses. They use a dig site to observe, record, categorize, and interpret what they find. Prehistoric archaeology deals with civilizations that did not develop writing. Artifacts from these societies may provide the only clues we have about their lives. While Archaeology can give us only a partial picture of the Celts, the evidence is free from the prejudice of Greco-Roman authors who saw the Celts as barbarians.

By putting all these sources of evidence together, we can build a plausible portrait of life in Celtic Gaul.

The Celts of Ancient Gaul is divided into eight sections:

- Introduction: How We Know about the Celts
- Chapter One: Brief Celtic Historical background (including Celtic Art)
- Chapter Two: The Celts in Gaul
- Chapter Three: The Raid: An Integral Part of the Celtic Social System
- Chapter Four: Kin-groups and Celtic Social Structures
- Chapter Five: Celtic Farming, Clothing, and Spiritual Beliefs
- Chapter Six: Caesar Invades Gaul
- Conclusion: Romanization

ERA		CULTURE	PEOPLE
Up to 4000BC		Early Stone Age	
4000-1800BC		Late Stone Age	
Bronze Age		Tumulus*	
		Early Urnfield	Indo-European
1000BC		Late Urnfield	
Iron Age	Hallstatt era		
	500BC	Hallstatt	Rise of the Celts and Illyrians
	La Tène era	La Tène	Celts
	15BC		

(Gerhard Herm, 1976)

*The Tumulus culture of the middle and late Bronze Age was widespread in Central Europe from 1450 to 1250 B.C. As the name implies, the Tumulus culture is distinguished by the practice of burying the dead beneath burial mounds (tumuli or kurgans). Grave goods include bronze ornaments (pins, spiral armlets, pendants), weapons, tools, and pottery with incised and stamped ornamentation. The Tumulus culture was eminently a warrior society of raiders and mercenaries and took control of peasant societies.

One

Brief Celtic Historical Background

The Celts who settled Gaul (France) were descendants from a group of people called Indo-Europeans, meaning they belonged to the same family of languages from which modern-day tongues such as English, Spanish, French, German, Hindi, Punjab, Persian, Italian, and Portuguese came . As discussed, within the Celtic linguistic group, there are two main branches: Continental and Insular. While Continental Celtic is extinct, Insular Celtic still exists as the distinct languages of Gaelic, Welsh, Scottish Gaelic and Breton (spoken in Brittany, France).

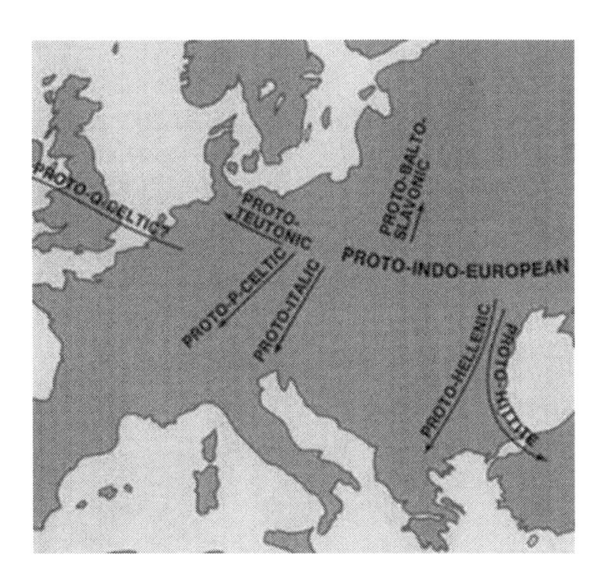

(Holly Burton, 1979 Penn Museum)

Indo-Europeans originally inhabited the vast grassland plains north of the Caspian Sea in Western Asia. Then about 3000 BCE, some of these stone-age tribes began migrating westward and southward, entering what is now Europe. By the late Bronze Age (the Bronze age spanned 3300 to 1200 BCE), many of these cultures had been replaced by the "Urnfield" people, who reached across a region extending from eastern France to Hungary and from Italy to Poland with a considerable degree of cultural uniformity. This period's name comes from the practice of burying the cremated remains of the dead in urns clustered in well-defined cemeteries. In addition to this, the varied array of personal ornaments, tools, and weapons, shows considerable stylistic similarities.

By 800 BCE, iron-working had replaced bronze-work-ing across most of the Urnfield region, which gave rise to the late Hallstatt culture (800 - 500 BCE). The name of this culture derives from the excavation undertaken near the village of Hallstatt, Austria, situated in the salt-mining region of Salzkammergat. (Before refrigeration, salt was instrumental in the preservation of meats.) Here, in the 1870s, a team of archeologists found more than 2,000 graves - containing both cremated and interred remains, along with caches of weaponry, armor, jewelry, and pottery decorated in an early Celtic "symmetrical" style. This period is regarded as the first clearly defined Celtic culture.

While it is difficult to re-create the social complexity of such a large region from archaeological evidence alone, it is safe to say the Celtic society was hierarchical (an elite class at the top who ruled over those below) as implied by the different quality of grave goods found throughout the period.

It appears the Hallstatt culture enjoyed six or seven centuries of stability where the population remained largely unchanged. The elite inherited ancestral territories in lines of unbroken succession going back for generations, while individual communities maintained a degree of harmony by long-established networks of obligation.

An assumed factor in allowing this was the culture's economic prosperity. Archaeological evidence indicates this early economy was primarily based on agriculture and maintenance of domesticated stock. Wheat and other cereal grains were subsistence staples and were supplemented with legumes, fruits, and berries, both wild and cultivated. Cows, pigs, sheep, and goats constitute the bulk of animal remains at Celtic settlement sites.

An interesting aspect of the Celtic economic society was clientship. This was the winning over and gaining the allegiance of individuals or groups belonging to other tribes in the chiefdom. Clients proved a valuable asset for any king in that he would loan them money and collect high interest in return. Clients also increased the size of the tribe making it less likely to fall victim from raids.

In addition to their agricultural activities, from its 1,312 feet deep mine shafts, the Hallstatt culture exported salt throughout Europe. Through its control of trade routes along the Danube River, the accumulated wealth facilitated the development of an advanced iron-making industry. With their iron ploughs, tools, and weapons, the Hallstatt people enjoyed a marked technological and military edge over other tribes. The raiding of neighboring Celtic and non-Celtic tribes for metal, farm animals, and slaves was common, but not a preoccupation.

Via the trade routes of the Rhône and Saône rivers valleys, the Hallstatt elites enjoyed a prosperous trade with the Greek city of Massalia (see cover, bottom right). One item that moved through Massalia and became a great part of the Celtic elite culture was wine. This also included such paraphernalia as flagons (a large container in which drink is served, typically with a handle and spout), large cauldrons (large metal pots with lids and handles) to hold and store wine, drinking cups, and kraters (large vases for wine). Wine was consumed mainly by the upper classes, leaving the lower classes to drink wheat beer, sometimes prepared with honey.

An observation about the Celts and wine by historian Diodorus from Sicily:

> The Gauls are exceedingly addicted to the use of wine and fill themselves with the wine which is brought into their country by merchants, drinking it unmixed, and since they partake of this drink without moderation by reason of their craving for it, when they are drunken they fall into a stupor or a state of madness. Consequently, many of the Italian traders, induced by the love of money which characterizes them, believe that the love of wine of these Gauls is their own godsend. They transported the wine on the navigable rivers by means of boats and through the level plain on wagons, and receive for it an incredible price; for in exchange for a jar of wine they receive a slave, getting a servant in return for the drink.

To protect both their wealth and trade routes passing through their kingdom, Hallstatt king-princes constructed earthworks called hillforts. A hillfort, essentially a defended enclosure, was an elevated site with ramparts (defensive walls) made from earth, wood or stone, and a ditch dug along the site's perimeter. The walls and ditches commonly followed the natural contours of the hill upon which the settlement was constructed. Many historians and archaeologists believe that the term 'hillfort' is misleading. It makes us think of castles and warfare, when we should be thinking in terms of 'enclosed places' built for a variety of purposes. While some hillforts were probably built with defense in mind, they may also have had ceremonial functions, and served as status symbols. As trade expanded and luxury items from the Mediterranean became available to the growing elite classes of Europe, hillforts grew in size and complexity (see oppidum Ch. 4).

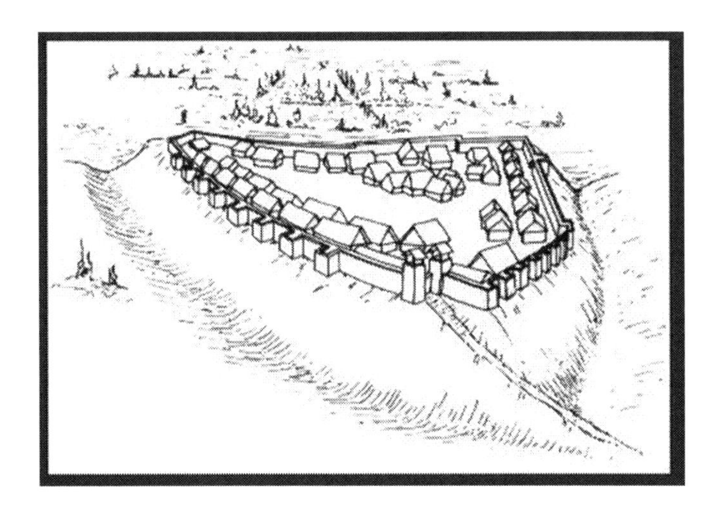

The control and accumulation of agricultural and metal products, valuable imported goods, wine, and rents were not only ways to increase one's power and authority, but a visible way to display one's high status. One's status was most apparent in burial customs. The tombs of the very wealthy chieftains and warriors were richly equipped with grave goods such as jewelry, fine weapons and armor, and fine tableware made of bronze, gold, and silver so that the king or warrior could display his superior wealth and status in this life and in the hereafter.

The Celts had no conception of heaven or hell as a reward or punishment for their conduct during life; rebirth into the afterlife was thought to be automatic. More importantly, they believed the afterlife (or Otherworld) would be much like this life and required grave or tomb offerings appropriate to their status. When it came to a chieftain or warrior, the cost of the items could be astronomical.

In nineteen sixty-eight, an amateur archaeologist discovered a richly furnished chieftain burial chamber near Hochdorf in Baden-Württemberg, Germany, dating from the Hallstatt culture period. What follows is the description from *The Celts* - BBC Series Ep 1 - " In the Beginning" found on YouTube.

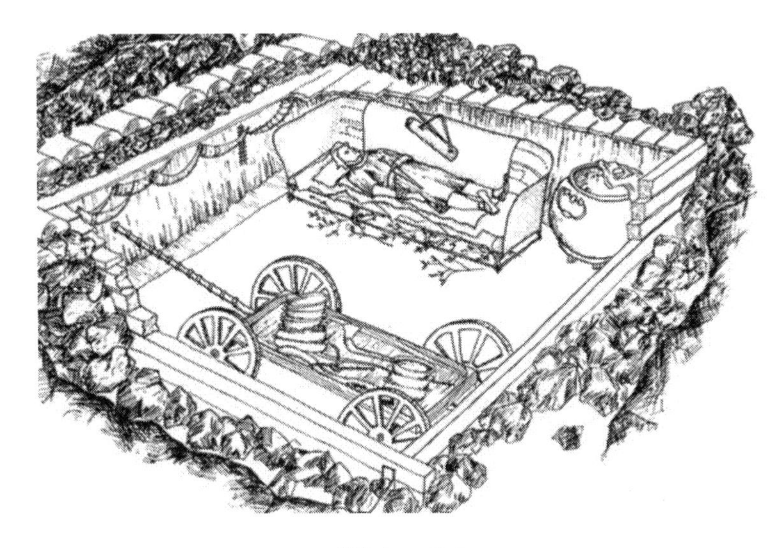

(Biel, 1987)

The corpse was adorned with a wide gold bracelet and a magnificently decorated dagger enclosed in fine gold. The Chieftain's torc, symbol of power and authority, worn around the neck, had been hammered from a single piece of gold. His shoes were adorned by thin gold plaques immaculately embossed. Over six feet two inches tall, his body was laid out on this bronze couch, which, at the time, was padded with animal furs. Pictured on the back of his four-wheeled burial wagon is a warrior—possibly depicting the very chief himself. The four-wheeled burial wagon was the most valuable object found. It took one modern-day blacksmith two years to reconstruct. This elaborate wagon sported a fine service of bronze dishes because there was to be a great welcoming feast in the other world. Nine places were set; according to the Greeks, nine was the ideal number for a feast. The Chief's drinking cup had been recreated to emphasize pleasures that await him in the hereafter. Now fully restored, the great wine cauldron in the tomb again shows the importance of the drinking and the feasting that lay ahead. The objects found in the Hochdorf Chieftain's grave show he represented a society whose aristocracy enjoyed great wealth.

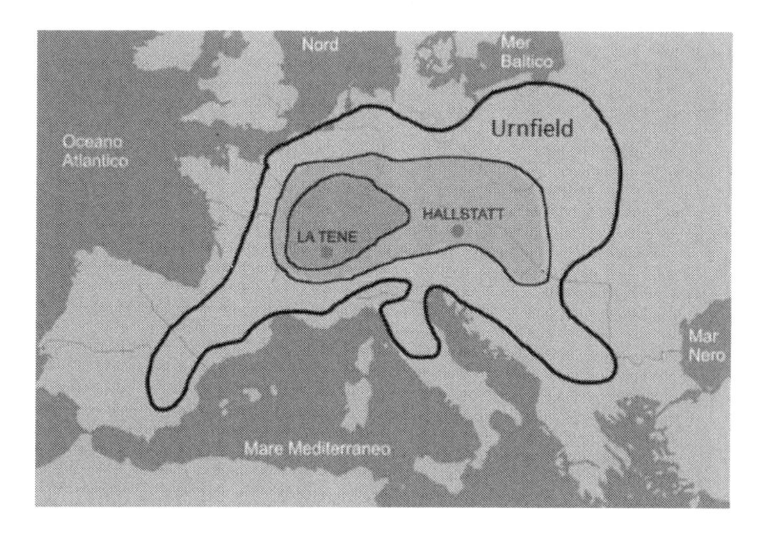

For reasons not fully understood, Hallstatt chiefdoms collapsed, giving rise to La Tène period. The new Celtic culture had its biggest impact on European culture beginning around 500 BCE. It was around this time the Celts began to expand out of their homeland throughout the rest of Europe. This period, which lasted some 300 years, is typically referred to as the "Celtic Migration," and is believed to be in part the result of overpopulation. (During this period, living conditions improved because salt allowed for meat to be preserved; iron allowed for stronger tools to clear thick forests and plow more land, and sharper scythes to cut grain.)

Also, a highly stratified society reliant on prince-kings giving “prestige goods” (gifts) to retain the loyalty of nobles may have been unable to maintain itself. (The factor behind this was probably the virtual halt of trade with Massalia, due to Carthage taking control of shipping and trade in the Mediterranean.) Besides having to obtain more and more goods for subordinates, more and more goods were demanded for the burial of rulers upon their death, leaving little or no wealth for the surviving tribe. Seeing the poor prospects that lay ahead, members of the warrior class may have thrown off their prince-kings and convinced large numbers of followers to migrate in hopes of discovering new profitable homelands.

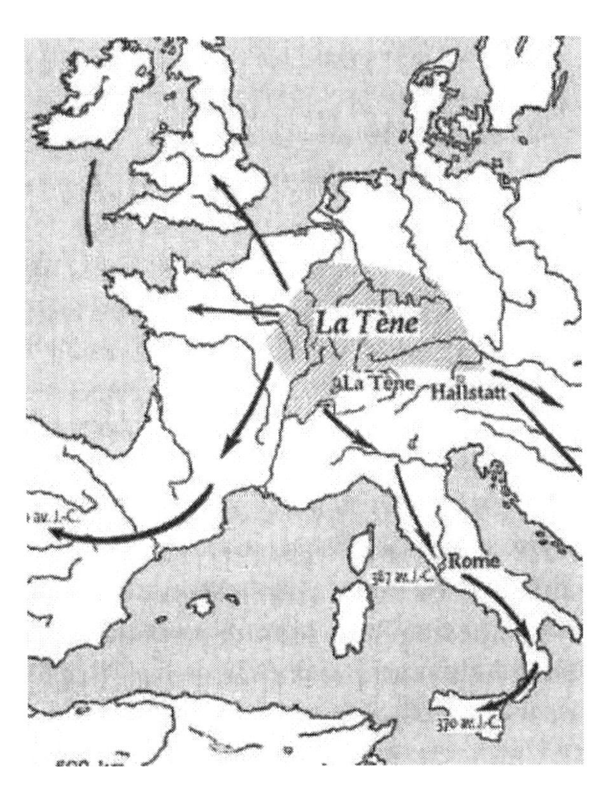

(Raftery, 2006)

During this migratory period, the Celts began to make contact with the Romans. As you will soon read, the contact was less than friendly and would spur Rome into transforming its militias into the most powerful army of the time. The full consequence of this would be felt when Caesar decided it was time to include Gaul into the Roman Empire in 58 BCE.

Although the Celts were, in time, forced to retreat, this period of expansion is an important part of Celtic history whereby it marked the first time the culture of the Celts was recorded in written history. What follows is a small portion of the observations made by the Greek historian, Polybius, who chronicled the first authentic description of the Celts we have.

The Celts, being close neighbors of the Etruscans and associating much with them, cast greedy eyes on their beautiful country, and on a small ploy, suddenly attacked them with a large army and, expelling them from the plain of the Po River, occupied it themselves. On their first invasion they not only conquered this country but reduced to subjection many of the neighboring peoples, striking terror into them by their audacity. Not long afterwards, the Celts defeated the Romans and their allies in a pitched battle, and occupied, three days after the battle, the whole of Rome with the exception of the Capitol, because they were diverted by an invasion of their own countrymen, the Veneti (Celtic Indo-European people who inhabited northeastern Italy), and made on this occasion a treaty with the Romans, evacuated the city, and returned home.

Meanwhile the Romans re-established their power and again became masters of Latium (the region of central western Italy in which the city of Rome was founded and grew to be the capital city of the Roman Empire). Thirty years after the occupation of Rome, the Celts again appeared before Alba (an ancient Latin city in Central Italy) with a large army, and the Romans on this occasion did not venture to meet them in the field, because, owing to the suddenness of the attack, they were taken by surprise and had no time to anticipate it by collecting the forces of their allies. But when, twelve years later, the Celts again invaded in great strength, Rome had early word of it, and, assembling their allies, marched eagerly to meet them, wishing for nothing better than a decisive battle. The Celts, alarmed by the Roman advance and at disputes among themselves, waited until nightfall and then set off for home, their retreat resembling a flight.

After this panic, they kept quiet for thirteen years, and then, as they saw how rapidly the power of the Romans was growing, made a formal peace with them, to the terms of which they adhered steadfastly for thirty years. But then, when a fresh migration began among the Transalpine Celts, and they feared they would have a big war on their hands, they tricked the migrating Transalpine tribes by bribery and by pleading their kinship, to join them in their attack on the Romans.

They advanced through Etruria, with the Etruscans too uniting with them, and, after collecting a quantity of booty, retired quite safely from the Roman territory, but, on reaching home, fell out with each other about division of the spoil and succeeded in destroying the greater part of their own forces and of the booty itself. This is quite a common event among the Celts, owing to their excess in eating and drinking.

Part A: La Tène

The next and last phase of Celtic development was carried out during the La Tène period. La Tène refers to a shallow area at the northern end of Lake Neuenburg in Switzerland. Early, in 1858, the amateur archaeologist, Colonel Schwab, brought up almost 2000 swords, scabbards (protective coverings) fragments, spearheads, knives, axes, sickles, javelins, rings, pots and half a small arm-ring of dark blue glass, and tools. Many of them showed signs of decoration such as scholars had never seen, and soon experts were describing the finds as the first in-dependent artistic achievement of any significance north of the Alps since the Ice Age.

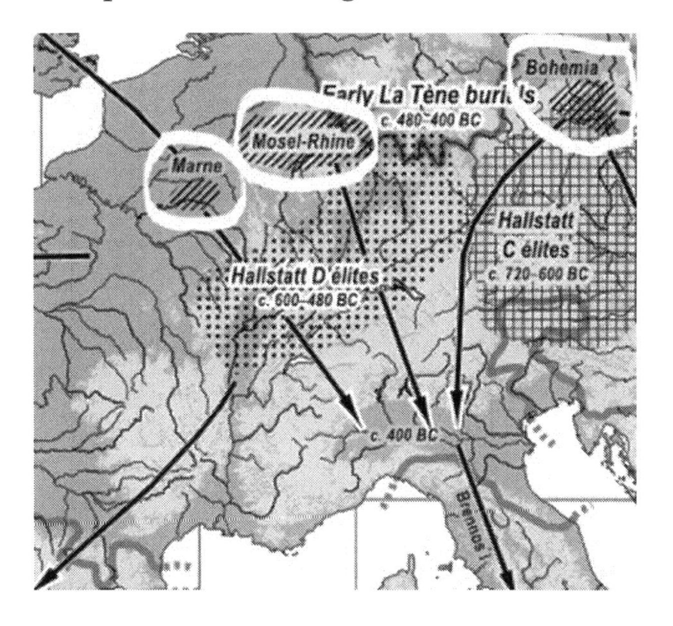

La Tène regions which brought rich rewards included Marne, Moselle, and Bohemia.

The originality of Gallic art showed a tendency towards the representation of human beings, animals, and fantastical and disturbing depictions of their gods. Artisans covered tiny surfaces of pots, swords and scabbards, and ornaments with a maze of lines, animal figures, and faces. De-tails were not merely suggested but chiseled out on an almost microscopic scale. Outstanding torcs (neck chains, see next page) contain marks smaller than a thumbnail, with fully modelled faces—arched eyebrows, googling eyes, bulb-like noses, and mouths turned down sarcastically at the corners.

(*France 24*, 2015)

Those words, 'La Tène', are a kind of shorthand for that period when the Celts were at the peak of the power and of their artistic achievement. It was an age typified by intricate Celtic art and craftsmanship and it was this art that has come to be seen as quintessentially Celtic. But beneath that romance and beauty there appears to be a much darker underbelly to the culture's savage customs and bloody brutality.

In places like Lake Neuenburg and other springs, wells, and rivers, people deposited weapons, and other kinds of objects, as offerings to the gods to commemorate victory in battle. Also, La Tène exposed a culture where war was a way of life and where beautifully crafted tools of battle were means of displaying a warrior's status.

These finds revealed a very different Celtic world from the two previous periods—one that was aggressive and warlike. It was also a world of stark contrasts in which beauty and creativity were entwined with cruelty and extreme violence.

Numerous Celtic art pieces can easily be found on the Internet.

Part B: La Tène

Celtic metalwork was the principal art form of La Tène, exemplified by many different classes of objects: from chariots, personal weapons and shields, to plows, equestrian fittings, and everyday implements like pitchers, mirrors, and razors. Personal adornments included head-dresses, bracelets, necklaces, torcs, rings, brooches, clasps, and amulets. All these items were made and decorated out of a variety of metals and other materials according to the importance of the customer or commission. Materials included gold, silver, bronze, copper, iron, amber, coral, ivory, bone, wood and of course iron. A range of pottery and ceramic art was also manufactured for both ceremonial and domestic use.

Celtic triskel. The three branches represent air, water, fire; the center represents the earth.

If the range of La Tène artifacts was comparatively narrow, the opposite was true of its design work, which featured an incredible diversity of ornamentation and pattern. La Tène designs used highly organic, curvilinear styles, with flowing curves and abstract leaf-like patterns. Common forms included (1) spirals (built up from S-shaped and C-shaped forms, among others); (2) knotwork; (3) geometric imagery, like the trumpet, the triskel (see left) and the palm, together with endless floral and plant shapes; (4) numerous shapes and pictures of animals, including: elephants, wild boars, wolves, stags, winged horses, bulls, hounds, cats, snakes, dragons, owls, and birds.

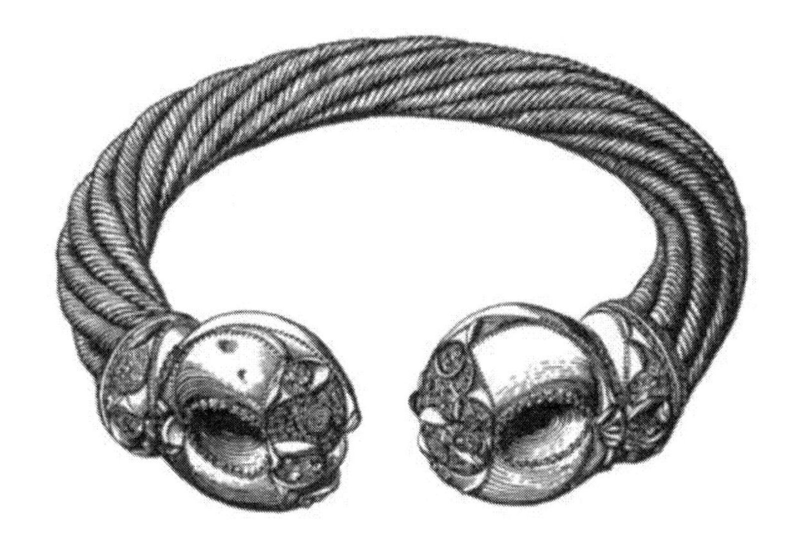

A Warrior's torc

As expected, grave sites became more elaborate and opulent, in keeping with greater prosperity among the chieftains and the emerging warrior class. This period of Celtic culture was more militaristic, and its burial sites reveal an abundance of swords, spearheads, shields and protective armor. The most obvious difference is the appearance of the two-wheeled warrior chariot instead of the previous four-wheeled burial wagon.

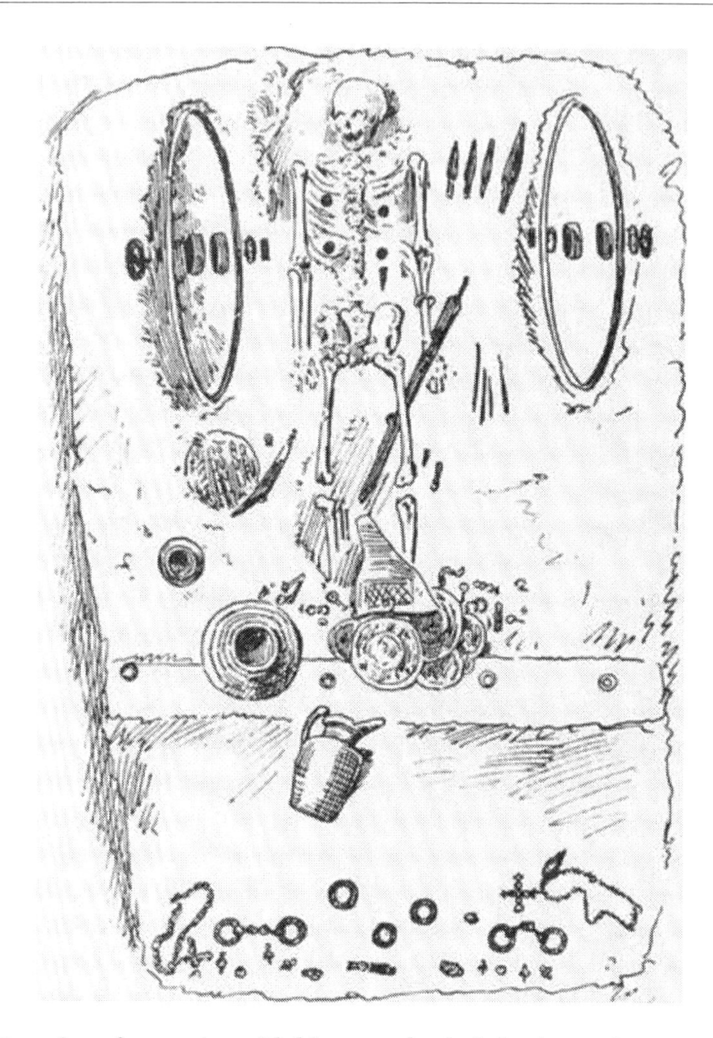

Remains of a warrior with his two-wheeled chariot and weapons
(The Celtic World, 1995)

In Western Europe, La Tène evolution and historical development reflected the fate of the Celts themselves. It achieved its zenith during the expansion of Celtic power and influence during the fourth century BCE and then declined with the Romanization of Gaul around 52 BCE. Its decline was reflective of the political weakness of the Celts themselves. Despite the ferocity of their warriors in battle, their loose network of tribal societies lacked the internal cohesion and central authority to compete with the unified Roman state.

Two

The Celts in Gaul

The conquest of Gaul by the Celts seems to have occupied the whole of the fifth century. Moreover, the whole Celtic nation did not invade Gaul. Part of it remained on the right (east) bank of the Rhine River. Between the Rhine and the Pyrenees Mountains, the Celts found various groups of the Ligurians. In regard to the national affinities or origin of the Ligurians themselves, we are almost wholly in the dark. Greek historian, Strabo, tells us they were of a different race from the Gauls or Celts who inhabited the rest of the Alps, though they resembled them in their mode of life.

The Ligurians were apparently an indigenous collection of Neolithic peoples living in village settlements in remote places. Archaeological remains indicate that livestock raising and primitive farming were the chief occupations. Yet, Strabo wrote, "The physical type, however, of the Ligurian differed as widely as possible from that of the Celt or Gaul, for the Ligurian was of small stature, nervous and wiry, far more capable of enduring fatigue than the 'Gaul,' whose huge, soft body melted away like wax before the scorching sun of Italy and Provence. In a stand-up fight, a Ligurian was considered a match for a Gaul twice his size. At field labor the Ligurian men and women alike were renowned for their endurance."

The Ligurians never formed a centralized political structure; instead they divided themselves into independent tribes living in small villages or castles. Rarely did they join together to fend off a common enemy. There were no dynastic leaders either; the Ligurian "king" was elected as leader of a tribe or a federation of tribes.

The territory of a tribe was almost entirely public property; only a small percentage of the land (the cultivated) was "private." Within the tribes, an egalitarian and communal spirit prevailed: women took part in the work of toil alongside men, and the women chose each other's husbands, demonstrating an emancipation unknown to other Indo-European cultures.

In pre-Roman times, the Ligurians occupied present-day Italian regions of Liguria, Piedmont south of the Po river, north-western Tuscany, and the French region of Provence

When the Celts migrated to Gaul, they found themselves a minority compared with the native Ligurians. While the Celts were triumphant, the slow nature of their conquest bears witness to the smallness of their numbers. They came with their wives and children and their spoils of war, which they bore in their train in long lines of chariots and wagons.

The conquerors and the conquered apparently intermingled very quickly. In primitive times, when social distinctions hardly existed, and civilization was still in an embryonic condition, similarities between religions and practices helped in the fusion of the two races into one homogeneous whole.

Furthermore, the spread of particular aspects of cultures do not necessarily mean a spread of people. Ideas have a life of their own. It is rare to find examples where the appearance of a particular 'cultural group' is closely tied to a mass migration of people. This new approach to archaeology stresses the importance of 'networks of communication,' where mobility of individuals—rather than of whole populations—was crucial. Ideas, or whole cultures, could emerge anywhere and spread through the network. As tempting as it might be, we do not need to invoke the expansion of a particular tribe to explain the spread of the Celtic culture.

The La Tène Culture in Gaul

By 500 BCE, most of Gaul had a recognizable Hallstatt-like culture, but this was quickly displaced by the more militaristic La Tène culture. The rise of the La Tène culture may indicate a period of greater conflict but may also have been due to the influence of neighboring Celtic tribes. As one tribe adopted a more hostile outlook, surrounding groups would tend to do likewise out of self-preservation.

Despite this, Celtic society was built around a social structure that provided stability. Although violent disputes were not uncommon, the Celtic social order kept these within acceptable limits and prevented society from breaking down. Without a stable society, even basic economic activities such as farming and hunting would be disrupted, resulting in a reduced ability to support the population.

La Tène I (475-300 BCE) is well represented in the northeast of France, especially in Champaign, where rich soils attracted a large Celtic population. Most graves are flat, with the skeleton extended on its back and accompanied by weapons or jewelry, while offerings of food were arranged in pottery vessels. The richest and most interesting of the burials are the *tombe à char*, in which the deceased, chief or warrior, is inhumed on a two-wheeled war chariot. Although about 100 *tombe à char* can be listed, precise details of possible grave goods fell victim to the greed of grave robbers.

La Tène II (300-100 BCE) is less well represented in France, because of migrations caused by pressures from the tribes known as the Belgie (Belgium) encroaching on Celtic territory. The disruption in trade with Massalia due to Carthage taking control of shipping and trade in the Mediterranean may have been another factor. Such migrations lead to the invasion of northern Italy and perhaps Greece and Asia Minor. Cremations became more common during La Tène II, and *tombe à char* were rare but more widely distributed.

La Tène III (100-52 BCE) brought radical changes in all fields: lowland settlements were abandoned in favor of upland oppida; cremations became the general rule; there were new items of armament and dress; and the wheel-turned pottery included innovations such as the 'Roanne painted pottery' with geometric or animal or floral motifs. (Hallstatt pottery was mostly of lines running from top-to-bottom.)

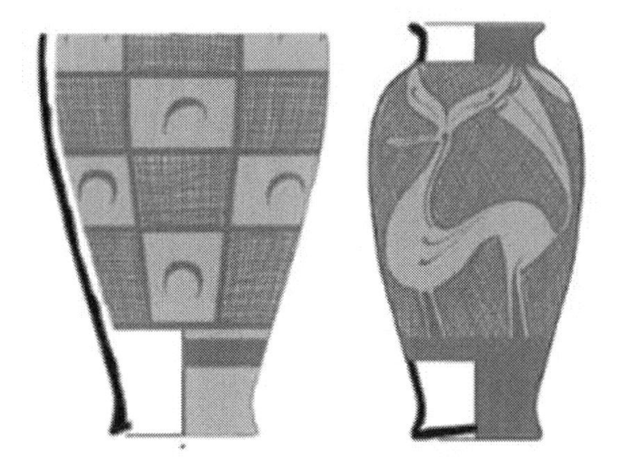

(Matthew Loughton, 2005)

La Tène III stopped abruptly in 52 BCE, the date of the battle of Alesia, which ended with the defeat of the most celebrated of Gallic chiefs, Vercingetorix. That defeat left Gaul at the mercy of Caesar's armies, and marked the end not only of a distinct and important period of history, but of the culture.

A new Gallo-Roman culture was created and lasted until the Barbarians (Huns, Franks, Vandals, Saxons, and Visigoths) invaded the region.

Three

The Raid: An Integral Part of the Celtic Social System

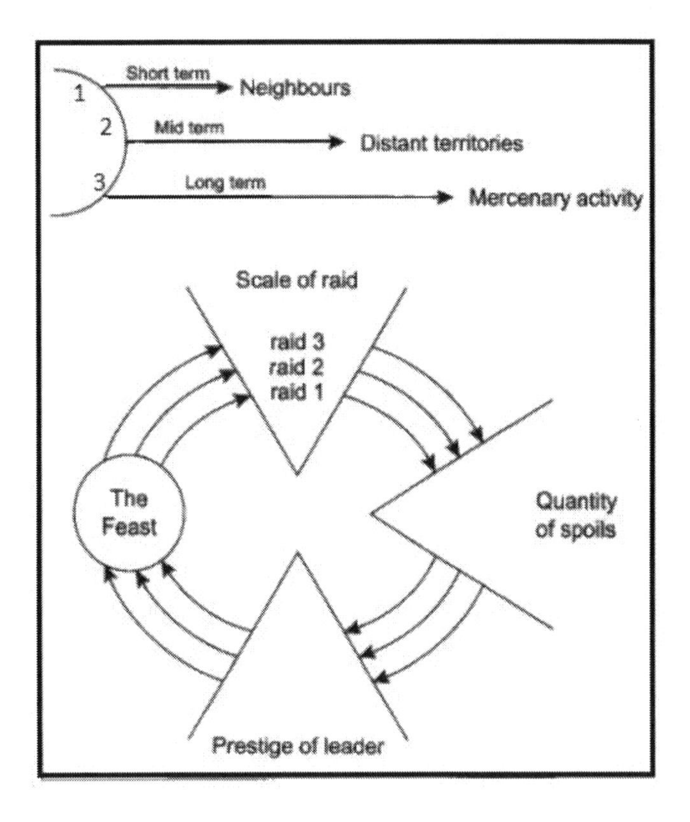

(Barry Cunliffe, 1997)

With the rejection of the prince-kings for the warrior-kings, the raid became an integral part of the Celtic social system. For a Celtic warrior to enhance his status, it was necessary to engage in acts of prowess—to demonstrate his ability to lead, to display acts of valor, and to acquire booty and prestigious goods for distribution in displays of generosity. Once the raid had become an established part of the status system, there was an inherent drive to intensify.

A successful raid with spoils to distribute provided increased status for the leader so that on the next occasion he would attract more followers. Younger men, wishing to aspire to greatness, would feel compelled to compete, and so the cycle would feed itself, growing all the while. In such a situation it is easy to see how the limited raid on neighbors would give way to more adventurous expectations, and how, for some sectors of the community, raiding became a full-time occupation.

Most battles between tribes would likely have been minor conflicts. They usually occurred as armed attacks on a neighboring tribe, since this kind of robbery was common practice and rewarded the respective leader with honor and glory.

It was also common only for the kings of each tribe to face off. Once one king was killed, the conflict was over. In these intra-tribal conflicts, cattle, gold, women, children, clients, and severed heads were highly prized as booty. Control of tribal territories seldom changed hands.

Time-honored Celtic combat was with long swords, whose weight and length provided the momentum to make them ideal for slashing and hacking. When fighting in loose formations, the Gauls were able to use their unique skills and strengths to the utmost. However, when fighting against Roman legions, with their discipline and tightly packed formations, the Gauls were deprived of space and found it difficult to wield their swords. This outdated battle tactic allowed the Romans to get in close and stab with their short swords. More so, the Gauls tended to fight with wild abandon rather than caution and discipline. This made them vulnerable to counterattacks, flanking maneuvers, and orderly retreats.

GALLIC WARRIOR.

In combat, status determined what one wore: 1) Some went into battle naked, showing off their bodies and their fearlessness in the face of man and nature. 2) Kings and higher-ranked warriors dressed in elaborate armor, displaying their wealth and status. Commonly worn by nobles was the torc, which not only displayed one's status, but also held deep religious significance—giving the wearer the sense of being protected by the gods. Their armor consisted of chain-mail shirts (which the Celts invented) and iron or bronze helmets. In some cases, helmets had large metal horns attached, while others had fearsome metal birds or beasts giving the appearance of enormous stature to the wearer. 3) Non-nobles would have fought in their usual everyday clothing, equipped with a sword and shield.

(Wikimedia Commons)

Celtic shields were usually oval, elongated, or hexagon shaped. On the front was a hollow wood shield boss [rounded bulge] to protect the hand. On the inside of the boss hole was a handle to hold the shield. Shields were made of wood, usually oak and often covered with leather.

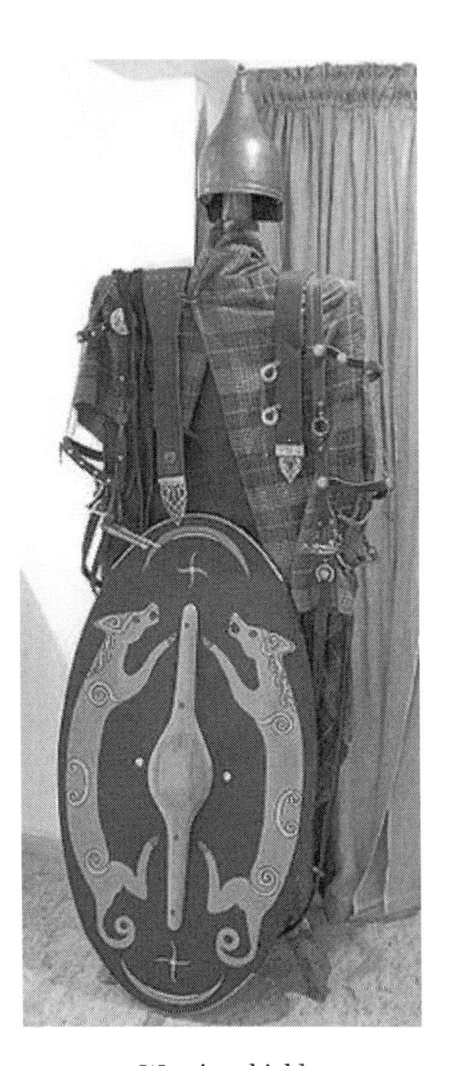

Warrior shield
(Wikipedia)

Battle shields were often individually decorated with various symbols. They were designed to be both light and strong. Celts used their shields defensively but also as an offensive weapon. A favorite tactic of a Celtic warrior was to strike the enemy with his shield.

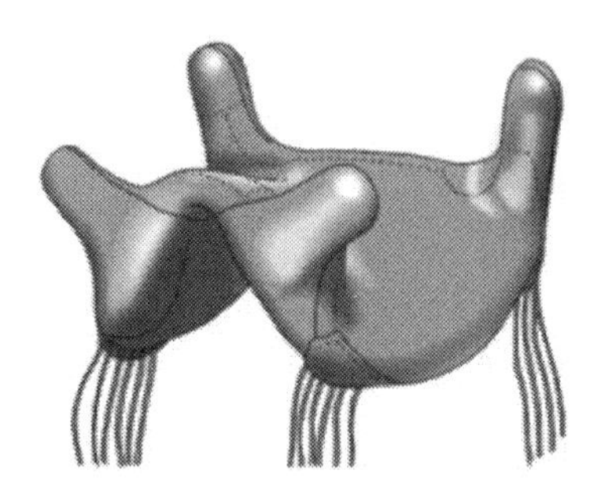

(Simon James, 2018)

While war chariots had been used through much of Celtic history, there was an absence of any reference to chariot warfare during Caesar's campaigns in Gaul. Instead, the wealthiest Gauls equipped themselves with horses to form cavalries. Although they did not have stirrups, the design of their saddles created a secure seat from which to thrust with a spear or hack with a sword. This was achieved by means of four tall pommels, two behind the rump and one tilted back over each thigh. Thereby, the rider sat in, rather than on the saddle. Around the third or second century BCE, the calvary became one of the most powerful arms of Gallic warfare.

Once a tribe came into contact with its intended foe, both sides deployed into lines of battle. Then as the battle approached, the warriors created a huge clamor of war cries, battle-songs, boasts and taunts, to which was added the fearsome sound of the *carnyx* or animal-headed battle horn.

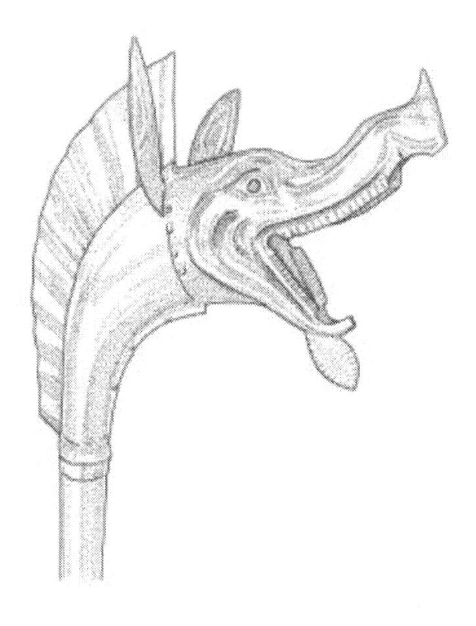

(Simon James, 2018)

YouTube:

"The Voice of the Carnyx (Ancient Celtic music)"

This is a recommended video because it also includes numerous images of Celtic warriors.

"Celts: Secrets of the Carnyx"

Musician John Kenny reveals the secrets of the Deskford carnyx, an Iron Age war trumpet that dates from 80-200AD.

With such a ruckus, it did not take long for all the warriors to be worked into a frenzy, often helped with large quantities of wine they mostly likely consumed.

As discussed previously, when regions became over populated, or when raiding or extravagant burials depleted a region of wealth, tribes migrated to distant territories. It was also common for Celtic warriors to go seeking their fortune as mercenaries which seems to have become a highly organized practice. Many warriors looked for fame and fortune in the rich, exotic Mediterranean world, in the hope of returning home with their reputations made. These mercenaries were quite willing to serve foreign masters, especially in the Greek states. Gauls from the Po Valley were recruited by Hannibal during the Second Punic War.

Central to the establishment and maintenance of the social system in the Celtic world was the feast.

The public dispersal of wealth in the form of gifts and elaborate feasts was how an individual's status was enhanced. The more that was given away, the greater the giver's reputation. At its most basic level, these gifts provided a simple redistribution mechanism by which surpluses could be spread throughout the community.

Besides the king and warriors, also in attendance were bards who would celebrate the lineage, bravery, and wealth of their patrons. Their songs, however, could either praise or satirize a king or a warrior, and fear of losing face in front of their guests encouraged kings and warriors to be even more generous than usual.

What follows is a description of a Celtic feast as recorded by the Greek historian Posidonius:

The Celts sit on cushions of wolves or of dogs, and have their meals served on wooden tables raised slightly above the earth. Their food consists of a small number of loaves of bread together with a large amount of meat, either boiled or roasted on charcoal or on spits. This food is eaten cleanly but like lions, raised up whole limbs in both hands and biting off the meat.

When a large number dine together, they sit around in a circle with the most influential man in the center, like the leader of the chorus, depending on whether he surpasses the others in warlike skills, or lineage, or wealth. Beside him sits the host and next on either side the others in order of distinction.

The servers take around the drink (wine) in earthenware or silver jars like spouted cups. They use this common cup, drinking a little at a time, but they do it rather frequently.

The Celts sometimes engage in small combat at dinner. They gather in arms and engage in mock battles, and fight hand-to-hand, but sometimes wounds are inflicted, and the irritation caused by this may even lead to killing—unless the bystanders restrain them.

Certainly, each occasion demanded another fresh banquet in return, this time given by the guest, or the most boastful warrior. And the only way for a guest to reciprocate, or for a warrior to live up to his boasting, was to stage a raid.

Four

Kin-groups and Celtic Social Structures

By the middle and later Iron Age, Celtic societies consisted of small territorial-based tribes which were the bases of public, civil, or military life. These were essentially kin-groups—extended families and clans—which attracted followers and dependents such as slaves and clients.

A tribe's territory generally corresponded with a small natural feature – plain, valley, plateau, or area surrounding a lake or hollow. But while this territory was primarily shaped by geography, each landform held a sacred dimension and became the theater of tribal mythology.

Large Celtic tribes probably started as small kin-groups and annexed surrounding families, forming kingdoms or chiefdoms claiming a common descent from a famous warrior, deities, or assumed qualities. In principle, while kingdoms were self-contained units, the integrity of joining or annexing tribes was not to be impinged upon. In other words, both the overlord king and lesser kings remained responsible for managing affairs within the bounds of their *kin-group*, which included enforcing laws internally and negotiating external affairs with their peers who ruled other groups.

A Celtic king was elected by the kin of the former king, meaning the eldest son did not necessarily become the successor to his father. It was necessary for the survival of the people to have a strong man on the throne, strong in mind as well as strength: a king who could defend his people against any threat from without or within. So the man who showed fitness for the post could be a younger son of the king, the king's brother, or even an uncle. Once a king achieved the throne, he was king for life, unless something like sickness or injury made him unfit to rule.

In Gaul, the nobility increasingly grew resentful of being excluded from religious, warrior, and judicial functions reserved for the king. Collectively, they abolished kingships for magisterial rule. As would be expected, usurped ruling royalty held out hopes of reclaiming their place. To prevent this, laws were passed to place power in the hands of an elected magistrate or *vergobret*. A magistrate's term lasted only one year, but his duties were very similar to that of a king. Like a king, a magistrate decided upon everything and even possessed the right of life and death; however, he could not lead an army. Military power was conferred upon a second official—generally a former *vergobret*. Everything was therefore so arranged as to avoid a *coup d'état* or return to kingships.

Celtic tribes had privileged classes of nobles, warriors, and individuals with special skills which included druids, seers, and bards. The druids played a vital role in maintaining the identity and well-being of the people, and the tribe's relations with the gods, the dead, and other communities. Seers, known in Gaul as *vates*, made predictions based on rituals or dreams. Bards shared with priests the role of a living repository of oral tribal history and traditions.

The most important social institution which structured the relationship between individuals of different status in society was that of 'clientship.' This was a relationship which embraced social, military, political, and economic obligations, and was seen as lying at the heart of the power of the nobility as well as conferring benefits on the client.

Although there were obligations on both sides, the relationship was fundamentally an unequal one. The patron provided his clients with legal support, political protection, and the possibility of sharing in the fruits of his success, including raiding and looting. He also supplied his clients with land and essential tools and equipment for farming. In return, the client paid the patron an annual food-rent based on the size of his farm, as well as manual labor, political support, and military service.

Clientship also provided an opportunity for the economic success in farming to be put to use in the promotion of one's social standings, and was the most important mechanism for the exercise of power by one person over another.

Slavery was common in Celtic societies where slaves tended to be captured as children or teenagers by professional raiders or slavers and sold into homes of all social ranks. Because slaves lived and worked alongside their owners who were not responsible for the violence of their capture, they could generally form strong bonds with them. Those who survived into middle age could be freed from their servitude and be granted land on the property of their former owners, and their offspring could be enfranchised by the kin-group. On the other hand, slaves were one of the main commodities sold to the Roman and Greeks in exchange for wine. Furthermore, most of the slaves would have been Celts—captured from neighboring tribes during raids.

Another social institution of Celtic was fosterage. It was considered a great privilege to be the foster-parent of a child, usually granted by parents of a higher status to those of a lower status. Fosterage was arranged by contract and divided into three periods: birth to age seven; eight to age twelve; thirteen to age seventeen.

Fosterage allowed a child to learn valuable skills from specialists outside the immediate family. Another rationale, however, was to keep children safe from harm (murder or maiming) that could be inflicted on them by jealous siblings who were competing for the inheritance of power and wealth. Such conflict was bound to happen in families of children with more than one mother (i.e., wealthy freemen could have more than one wife and hence many eligible children).

Historians were right to place the origin of the tribe in the family. The tribe was generally designated by a proper name, a family name, or the name of the founding chief or some ancestor. The tribe was a collection of families and individuals rendering obedience to common kings, bound by one set of rules, leading a similar existence, and living as neighbors on the same territory. Each tribe had its own traditions, its protective deity, and common interest.

Each of the many tribes of Gaul were molded by the country [landscape] where they were located—imposing on successful generations a particular form of labor. Those regions with rich soil were dominated by farmers; woodcutters lived in wooded regions; boatmen and fishermen lived near rivers and lakes; land rich in minerals produced workers in metal; and where clay dominated the soil, 'pottering' became the dominant craft.

Each tribe had its own sanctuary, its place of refuge, its marketplace, in which the heads of the families met together, thus forming a headquarters or capital for the tribe. Over time these small clusters developed into an *oppidum*. An oppidum (plural oppida) was a large, defended settlement associated with the Celtic La Tène culture, emerging during the 2nd and 1st centuries BCE and spread across Europe. Often, an oppidum was simply the enlargement of a hillfort. Oppidum is a Latin word meaning the main settlement in any administrative area of ancient Rome. The word is derived from the earlier Latin *ob-pedum*, "enclosed space," and it was Julius Caesar who described the larger Celtic settlements he

Image courtesy PeriklisDeligiannis.Wordpress.com
(see site for more information.)

encountered in Gaul as oppida. Archaeologists define an oppidum as a site from 20 to over 1,000 hectares large (1 hectare=2.47 acres) that is entirely surrounded by fortifications, both natural (rivers, cliffs, and swamps) and constructed.

A typical oppidum was bisected by a main street that led from the main gate to a gate on the other end, with other streets crossing the main road. Workshops and craft areas would be clustered on the main road near the gate. There, bronze and iron smiths, the workers in bone and leather, as well as makers of fine pottery and glass would have their shops and sell their wares. Basically, oppida were places of public assembly and trade, where merchants congregated, animals and goods were bought and sold, and social and religious ceremonies took place.

Most oppida were built on an elevated position. Such a location would have allowed the settlement to dominate nearby trade routes and may also have been important as a symbol of control of the area.

Size and construction of oppida varied considerably. In western Europe, the *murus gallicus* construction type (Latin term for a 'Gallic wall' or rampart) was often used. This meant stone-faced construction with a timber and rubble core, in which the timbers were placed in horizontal layers, criss-crossing laterally and longitudinally.

(Wikimedia Commons)

The development of oppida was a milestone in Celtic urbanization as they were the first large complexes north of the Alps that could genuinely be described as towns. While hillforts could accommodate up to 1,000 people, oppida could reach as large as 10,000 inhabitants.

Five

Celtic Farming, Clothing, and Spiritual Beliefs

Iron Age Celtic society was essentially rural; most people spent their lives on the land, engaged in raising crops, tending herds, managing woodlands, and all the other tasks of the farmer's year. Without the goods produced by farmers, little else would have been possible. For instance, a warrior class could not be supported for long by the simple pillage approach.

The basic tool of all farming at the time was the plow, a tool that digs and cuts the earth so that crops can be planted. Early plows were too primitive to dig effectively, so most European societies practiced 'double plowing,' which entailed running the plow over a field twice to break the soil. This was difficult and time-consuming.

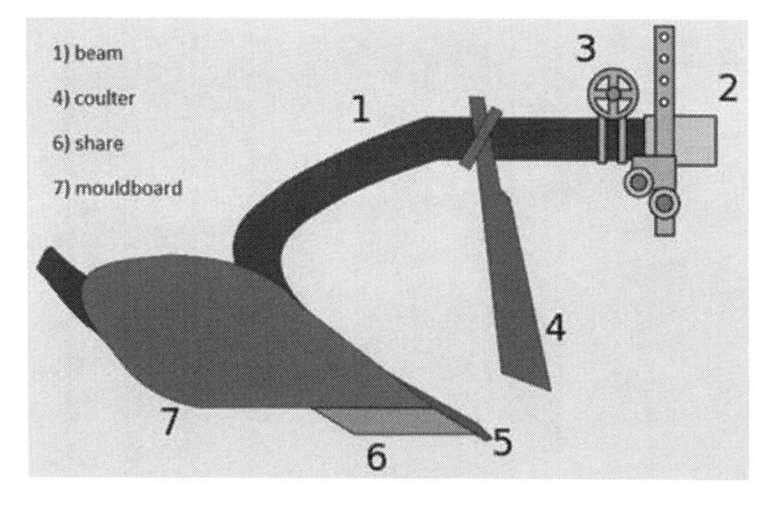

(Wikipedia)

To solve this problem, the Celts added a coulter, a sharp knife, to the plow beam. The coulter made a vertical cut through the soil at the same time as the blade of the plow, called a plowshare, made a horizontal cut. A moldboard [mouldboard], a curved iron plate was attached above the share to lift and turn soil over. In this way, the soil was turned over in one pass. This simple innovation drastically changed farming because fields could be plowed quickly and effectively. The Celts also began making plowshares out of iron, even as other cultures continued using wooden plowshares. This combination of metal coulter and plowshare made the job of preparing fields for planting much easier.

The introduction of iron also helped farmers in that sickles, scythes, spades, pitch forks, axes, and billhooks became more powerful and durable.

A billhook to cut grain
(backwoodshome.com)

The Celtic farmers grew a large variety of cereal crops, especially wheat, barley, and mullet. Legumes like beans, peas, and lentils were also cultivated, and from archaeological evidence, it has been found that a wide variety of fruits and berries were grown. For livestock, farmers relied primarily on sheep, cattle, and pigs. It seems sheep were raised for their wool, and perhaps milk, rather than meat. Flax was also grown for linen, as an alternative to wool, and probably for its oil.

For farmers of this period, harvesting was the most intense operation of the entire agricultural cycle. The main obstacle in increasing the harvesting rate was the impossibility of increasing the labor productivity by using human muscles only. It was the inventor of the 'Gallic reaper' who was first to conceive the idea of using draft animals for harvesting.

(Wikimedia Commons)

The Gallic reaper was a two-wheeled cart with a donkey, mule, or oxen yoked to its draw-bar frame. The animal pushed the cart forward from behind. The cart was shaped into a basket with a row of tapered teeth (comb) mounted in the front. The front edge of the basket's height was set slightly below the top of standing crop. One operator knocked grain into a basket with a stick while the second operator drove the animal and guided the mechanism.

Gauls also used field rotation, irrigation, and fertilizer. Throughout the Celtic world, the intensive exploitation of agricultural land required manuring to ensure the soil remained fertile. Classical writers attest to the fertilization of land by using lime and marl, which is a limey clay. Their wheeled carts and roads allowed them to deliver their goods to markets efficiently. (In the past, it was assumed the Romans were the first to construct roads throughout Gaul. However, recent archaeological discoveries have shown the Gauls had a very complete network of roads made of wood and it was over these roads the Romans laid their stones.)

Celtic Clothing

The Celts like bright colors for their clothes and wove checks and patterns into them, similar to Scottish tartans. Colors favored by the Celts were blue, red, and yellow, with various shades of gray. They used different materials according to their location. Leather, wool, and hemp have survived, as well as fibers made from animal hair. Men typically wore long trousers which often times were brightly colored, even striped. Celts also made quality leather shoes from a single piece of animal hide.

(Ancient costumes of all nations – British, Gallic and German, 1882.)

Females typically wore a long dress that has become known as a 'bog dress.' This rather uncomplimentary term derives from the fact that the dress was worn as a utility garment for all tasks including trips to a nearby bog to cut peat for fire.

Tunics of varied in length and design were also worn, Those who had to move freely in order to work wore a relatively short tunics or shirts, while those who could afford to stand around were able to wear longer tunics that might come down to the knees. Both genders wore tunics of various designs that were woven of wool or other fabrics, and even leather. There is some evidence that more than one tunic might be worn at a time when more waterproofing or warmth was needed.

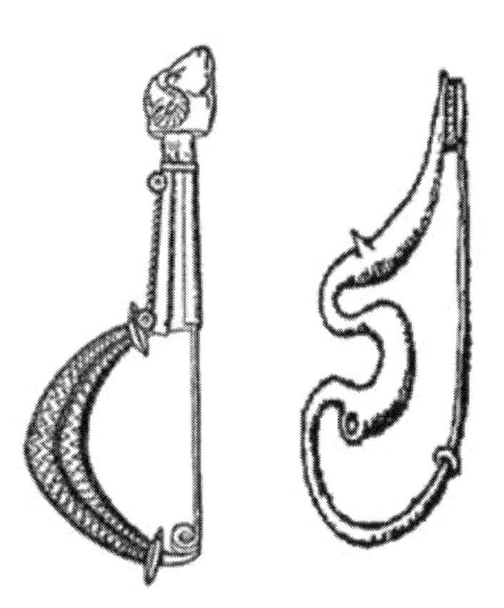

Clothes were fastened together by means of brooches. Those from the Champagne district of eastern France were of a relatively simple design, whereas the people in Central Europe wore a whole series of these ornaments called "mask fibulas." Here Celtic craftsmen gave free rein to their imagination, combining fabulous animals with human shapes that bordered on caricature in a surrealistic way. Representations of heads seem to have had a magical or religious purpose as well as an aesthetic one.

Celtic Spiritual beliefs

The Song of Amergin

This oral poem hails from the time before the Roman invasion of Ireland. Amergin is a god-like bard and the poem reflects his supernatural persona.

I am the wind on the sea;
I am the wave of the sea;
I am the bull of seven battles;
I am the eagle on the rock;
I am a flash from the sun;
I am the most beautiful of plants;
I am a strong wild boar;
I am a salmon in the water;
I am a lake in the plain;
I am the word of knowledge;
I am the head of the spear in battle;
I am the god that puts fire in the head;
Who spreads light in the gathering on the hills?
Who can tell the ages of the moon?
Who can tell the place where the sun rests?

(Translated by Lady Gregory, Wikipedia)

The picture painted by the evidence is of a rich and varied Celtic religious tradition. This variety and complexity is due largely to the essential animism which appears to have underpinned Celtic religion—the belief that every part of the natural world, every feature of the landscape, was mystical and possessed a spirit. These natural forces were perceived as capable of doing humankind good and harm, so they had to be controlled and their power harnessed by means of insight, sacrifice, and appeasing rituals.

Religious practice varied from region to region with different tribes worshipping different gods. Yet we can identify common features of Celtic beliefs. Their gods were both male and female. Female deities represented aspects of a supreme Earth-mother goddess. Male gods were more concerned with the worldly affairs of the tribe, such as the all-important business of war.

The Earth-mother goddess was not only a deity; she was the physical representation of earth and its powers to give life. She appears to have supplied most gods of the Celtic pantheon. Dis Pater was widely regarded as her son, to whom the dead returned in death. Dis was originally associated with fertile agricultural land and mineral wealth, and since minerals came from underground, he was later equated with Pluto (ruler of the underworld in classical mythology). Also, all Gauls claimed to be descended from Dis.

The Earth-mother probably entered the Celtic culture with the development of agriculture. Over time, due to man's constant preoccupation with the growth and storage of food for man and beast, related rites emerged. In hunting and agricultural life, these rites became intimately associated with daily life. And what was true with those above was also true, in a greater or less degree, in the life of the Celtic metal-worker or the Celtic warrior.

Each tribe would have had its own divine father. He would be thought of as the ancestor of the people, the father of the king in whom so much divine power was believed to reside. The father-god would preside over justice and laws in time of peace, and would take up arms and lead his people into battle in times of war.

Trees were especially revered by the Celts. Nemetona, goddess of the tree grove, was an important deity because many religious ceremonies were conducted in sacred groves. It was common for trees to be hung with offerings or with the heads of victims. The historian Pliny said of the Celts: "They esteem nothing more sacred than the mistletoe and the tree on which it grows. But apart from this they chose oak-woods for their sacred groves and performed no sacred rite without using oak branches." Also, according to Pliny, mistletoe was believed to have general powers of healing, was an antidote for all poisons and could overcome infertility.

The Celts did not worship their deities and perform their religious rights only in sacred groves. They were known to construct earthworks or timber-built temples and use ritual poles or pillars as the focus points for sacrifices and ceremonies. Many tribes utilized shafts, pits, wells, and lakes for the disposal of sacrificed animal and human, and votive (an offering in fulfillment of a vow) to their gods.

Animals in Celtic mythology were connected with fertility and vitality, because they are living, moving, and growing. They also provided vitality and continued life for the tribes through their meat, skins, and bones. This spiritual connection to animal spirits and gods was played out through their assistance in the hunt, and their imparting of secrets and wisdom. Major animals included the bull, the stag, and the hunting dog, with the boar most sacred of all. Birds also played a vital and basic role in Celtic religious imagery. Water birds of every kind were associated with the sun's healing aspects. The sun itself was represented as being pulled across the sky by a duck or goose.

The Celts believed strongly in the idea of metamorphosis. Many myths and legends tell of gods and goddesses who changed into the forms of birds and animals. To them, a crow flying overhead was more than a bird—it might also be a goddess speeding away on some urgent errand. Druids drew omens from birds in flight and bird calls. An angry, snorting boar was an animal, certainly, but it might also be an enraged god.

Epona, meaning "Divine Mare", was the goddess of horses. Her worship originated with nomadic Celts in Gaul and extended throughout Continental Europe and the Roman Empire. Celtic nobles were usually buried with their horses and saddles, signifying the importance of horses in the after-life. The extensive worship of Epona may also be the reason why the Celts did not eat horse meat. Epona was the only Celtic deity venerated in Rome itself.

The Celts believed the power of nature flowed around them at all times. It could be seen not only in trees and animals but also in specific natural geographic locations. One of the most powerful places in the Celtic world were areas associated with water. The Celts understood that water was the basis of life and its ability to give life to plants, animals, and people.

Anne Ross, in her discussion on the subject writes, “Springs, wells, and rivers were of first and enduring importance as a focal point of Celtic cult practice and ritual. Rivers were important in themselves, being associated in Celtic tradition with fertility and with deities such as the divine mothers and the sacred bulls concerned with this fundamental aspect of life.”

Spring water was thought to possess healing powers. Wells, lakes, and pools were the sight of ceremonies where valuable treasures (long iron swords, lanceheads, heavy knives, knot-work, metalwork, pottery) would be deposited as votive offerings to the gods. The famous La Tène archaeological site, for example, was one such offerings place. The present practice of throwing coins into fountains draws its inspiration directly from this practice.

The names of more than four hundred Celtic gods and goddesses have been recorded by historians. These deities cared for the land and the people, and in return, the Celts worshipped them. However, each tribe had its own local gods, so it was up to the druids to make sense of the group's local gods and the beliefs associated with them.

The Celts saw years as being another aspect of the natural world filled with darkness and light, birth and death, warm and cold. The four Fire Festivals marked the turning of the seasons. Two of the fire festivals, Samhain and Beltane, were considered to be male, and Imbolc and Lughnasadh were female.

The greatest festival was Samhain (SOW-an), observed on November 1st but celebrated the night before. Samhain was the Celtic New Year and marked the end of the summer growing and grazing season, and the time when cattle and sheep were brought together and slaughtered.

Samhain was also a time between the old and new year when Celts believed spirits from the Otherworld could walk on earth. Magical powers were very powerful during this and many important rituals were conducted. Today, remnants of the Celtic beliefs can be seen in the Halloween celebrations that include spirits and ghosts.

The first female festival was Imbolc, which literally means "in milk", traditionally marking the lactation period of ewes and cows. Ewes are unable to produce milk until after they bear their young, which occurs at this time. Since milk was very important to the basic survival of the tribes, this was a time of great joy. It meant the end of a long winter was in sight, and green pastures were only a few months away.

During the Imbolc ritual it was customary to pour milk (or cream) onto the earth. This was done in thanksgiving, as an offering of nurturing, and to assist in the return of fertility and generosity of the earth to its people (the return of Spring).

The second male Celtic celebration was Beltane. This holiday, celebrated on May 1st, marked the arrival of the light months of spring and summer. The word "Beltane" literally means "bright" or "brilliant fire," and refers to the bonfire lit by a presiding druid. It was a fertility celebration, filled with feasting and dancing. It also corresponded with the release of cattle for grazing in the field. Today some people in Europe continue to celebrate May Day with gifts of flowers, and the tradition of dancing around a Maypole which harks back to the ancient Celtic Beltane celebrations.

Lughnasadh was a summer festival lasting for as long as two weeks either side of the day itself, which fell around July 31st. It marked the beginning of the harvest season, and the decline of Summer into Winter. It typically centered around the assurance of a bountiful harvest season and the celebration of the harvest cycle. A bountiful harvest ensured the safe passage of the tribe through the upcoming winter months. Lughnasadh was celebrated to honor the God, Lugh, who was associated with both the Sun and agricultural fertility.

The Celt's idea of immortality was that death was but a change of place where life went on in all its forms to the fabulous Otherworld. When people died in the Otherworld, however, their souls were reborn in this one. Celts, then, regarded death in this world with joy because it led to their birth in the Otherworld, and mourned birth because it meant returning to this world.

So firm was the Celtic belief in the Otherworld they lent sums of money to each other which were repayable in the next world. In other words, they were convinced the souls of men were immortal. As discussed earlier, rich grave goods, personal belongings, weapons, food and drink were buried with the dead to give them a good start in the Otherworld.

Because the Celts believed the soul resided in the head, the taking of an enemy's head was a way to appropriate his spirit and qualities. A severed head also served as a trophy testifying to the military prowess of the victor. It was a mark of great prestige to take the head of a respected warrior, embalm in cedar oil, and display for all to admire.

The Celts, like many other "barbarian peoples," hunted human heads. It was found in antiquity among the Germans, Scyths, and the Romans who still practiced the custom at the height of the Gallic Wars. Therefore, it is wrong to interpret this as evidence the Celts were headhunters. Decapitation only took place after the victims were slain in battle, or died, and then only if they were deemed worthy of respect. Despite this, Diodorus Siculus couldn't help but comment:

When their enemies fall they cut off their heads and fasten them about the necks of their horses; and turning over to their attendants the arms of their opponents, all covered with blood, they carry the heads off as booty, singing a tribute over them and striking up a song of victory, and these first-fruits of battle they fasten by nails upon their houses, just as men do, in certain kinds of hunting, with the heads of wild beasts they have mastered. The heads of their most distinguished enemies they embalm in cedar oil and carefully preserve in a chest, and these they exhibit to strangers.

Six

Caesar Invades Gaul

By 60 BCE, before the Romans entered Gaul, there were already signs of a higher order of things. Tribes were merging into alliances covering much of Gaul. Some were striking coins with crude Greek letters. These "Gallic" Celts might have evolved into a real empire in a few hundred years — if they had been left alone.

They were not to be left alone. Shortly before the start of the 1st century BCE, Romans began moving into France. They referred to the region as "Gaul" and called the Celts "Gauls." Unlike the scattered Gallic tribes, who had no central government or national army, Rome was a well-organized nation with a large and efficient army. In 118 BCE, Romans established a colony on France's southern coast.

Julius Caesar

Soon, the Roman colony expanded into the large province of Narbonensis. The Roman intrusion into Gaul became a full-blown conquest in 58 BCE when renowned Roman leader, Julius Caesar, marched northward from Narbonensis. Over the next eight years, Caesar subdued Gallic tribes one by one.

Between 58-57 BCE, Caesar sent Publius Crassus and one legion deep into Northwestern Gaul to secure support from tribes with a nonviolent show of force. He also sent another legion, under the command of a legate named Galba, to the Alps. Galba's job was to set up permanent outposts which would protect travelers from the Gauls living in the mountains and to make it easier to transport goods in and out of Italy. While constructing one of these mountain outposts, Galba's legion was attacked by the native Gauls, and for a time, they were completely surrounded. However, Galba broke out in a surprise attack, which won him the day.

With one legion busy establishing a safe route through the Alps, and another legion was making peace with the tribes in Northwestern Gaul, Caesar convinced himself Gaul was "reduced to a state of tranquility." But Gaul's tranquility would not last long.

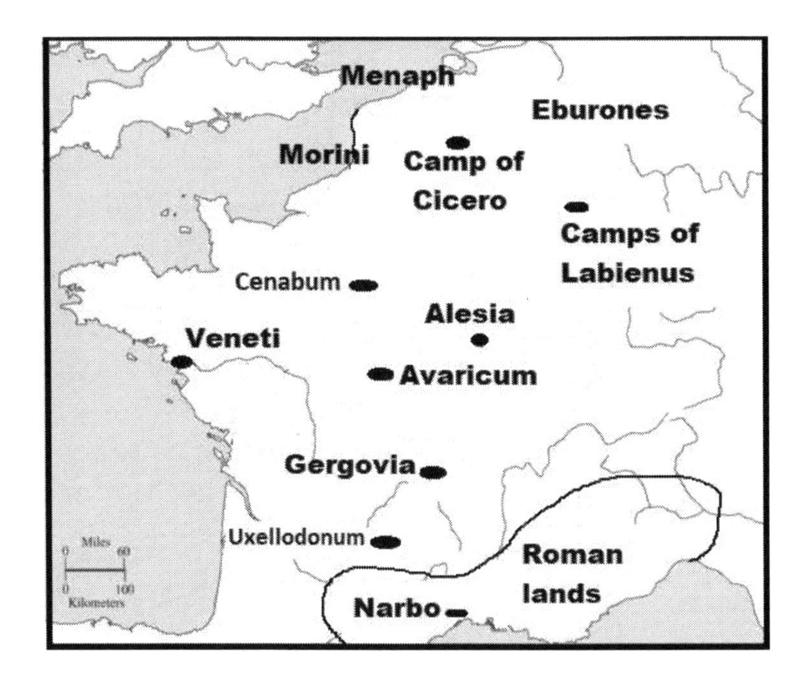

In Northwestern Gaul, Crassus had established diplomatic relations with many of the tribes in the region but took hostages to assure the terms of the relations were upheld. (Hostages weren't kept in cages; instead, they were used as collateral if anything undiplomatic happened.) Some of these hostages were from a tribe called the Veneti (seafaring Gallic people who lived in the Brittany peninsula, France). Crassus later sent diplomats to the Veneti to negotiate the purchase of some grain. When the Veneti learned of their enslaved tribe members, they arrested the Roman diplomats and took them as hostages of their own.

When Caesar got word of this, he interpreted this as an act of war. He immediately ordered a fleet of ships built on the Loire River that led to the Atlantic Ocean and mobilized his entire army. He then sent a message to Crassus telling him to move south and continue establishing contact with the tribes there.

With that done, Caesar ordered three fresh legions (each comprising 7,000 men) to northwestern Gaul to prevent neighboring tribes from aligning themselves with the Veneti. He then instructed his lieutenant, Labienus, to go with one legion to the newly pacified Belgae territory just in case they took this opportunity to try something. Caesar told his river-fleet to start rowing towards the Atlantic Ocean whenever they were ready, and with three legions, he marched off to confront the Veneti. (This would be the Battle of Morbihan Gulf at the mouth of the Loire river, 56 BCE.)

When the Veneti heard there were Romans coming their way, they loaded everyone onto their giant sailing ships and headed for safety. From just offshore, they watched as Caesar came across their abandoned villages and systematically burned them to the ground.

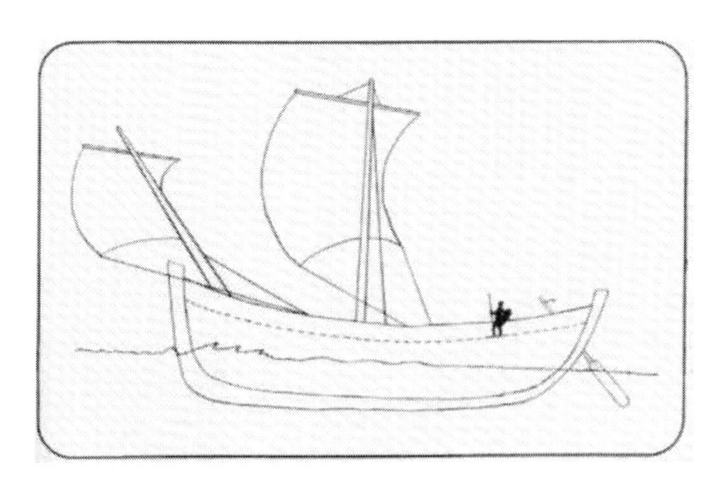

What a Veneti ship may have looked like.
Rome's Enemies (2): Gallic & British Celts
(Oxford: Osprey, 1985)

What the Veneti didn't expect was for a Roman fleet to appear out of nowhere. Roman oar ships were rather small, designed for going back and forth across the Mediterranean, while the Veneti ships were giant sailing vessels designed for long distance travel in the Atlantic Ocean. The Roman ships attacked, but they quickly discovered the huge Veneti ships were too sturdy to ram, with sides too tall to board. The Romans decided to pull up alongside them and pull down the Veneti rigging with big hooks on poles, preventing them from sailing away. After that, the Romans climbed onto the Veneti ships and set fire to them.

The fate of a defeated enemy depended entirely on the mood of the victor. This time Caesar was in a vengeful mood, and had the members of the Veneti senate executed, and the rest of the tribe sold into slavery. This unthinkably harsh punishment caused an uprising by some of the neighboring tribes, which were easily squelched by Caesar's three legions.

Caesar's final campaign of the year was less successful. The only tribes that had not yet acknowledged Roman authority were the coastal tribes of the Menapii, who lived in the Rhine–Meuse–Scheldt delta, and their western neighbors the Morini. As the Romans advanced towards the coast, the Menapii and the Morini withdrew into their swamps, thus, preventing their capture. Caesar had to make do with the destruction of some empty villages and then withdrew the south into winter quarters.

Julius Caesar spent two full years preoccupied with an expedition of Britain. While there, the political situation back in Gaul was in a state of flux. Leaders from rival Gallic tribes were holding meetings where they shared their concerns about the Roman presence. They were all convinced Caesar was preparing a full-blown annexation of Gaul. When a consensus was reached, the leaders agreed to secretly coordinate with one another when dealing with the Romans.

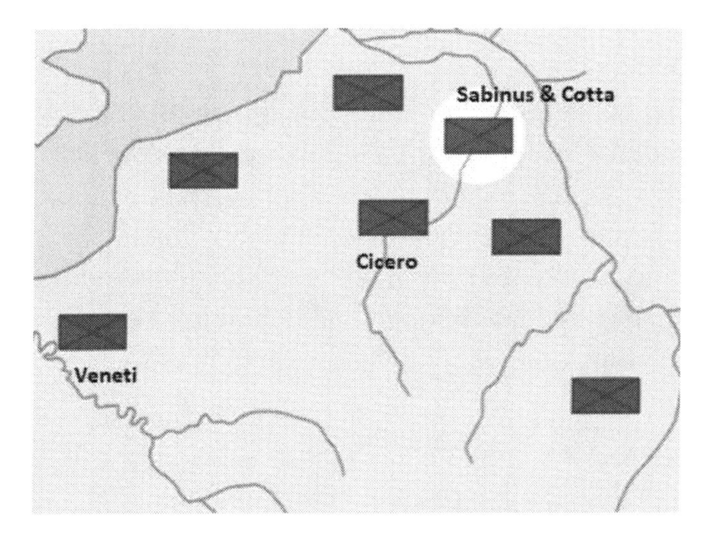

(Historia Civilis)

Before the snows came, Caesar divided his entire army into eight legions and sent them to winter with different tribes all over Gaul. One smaller legion (5,000 men) was sent to the Belgae territory near the Rhine River. It was under the joint command of the two legates Sabinus and Cotta. The troops arrived in the region and built their camp, settling in for the winter. A few days later, some soldiers were attacked by the Eburone Gauls while out gathering wood.

The camp quickly mobilized and chased the attackers off, but they didn't know what to make of it. They thought they were on good terms with the Eburone and their leader Ambiorix. Ambiorix then appeared at the gates of the Roman camp asking to parley. He told Sabinus and Cotta the area Gauls were secretly conspiring against the Romans, and he had been pressured into participating in a coordinated attack. Ambiorix continued by claiming other Gallic tribes were going to rise up and attack the nearby Roman legion. Ambiorix then told Sabinus and Cotta if they wanted to march to this legion's aid, he would guarantee safe passage through his territory.

On the first leg of the march, Sabinus and Cotta had to pass through a small valley. As they were midway through, Ambiorix appeared with his army. The whole thing had been a trick. The Gauls blocked both ends of the valley and then more Gauls appeared on the side hills—completely surrounding the Romans. Both Sabinus and Cotta, and most soldiers, were killed.

Many tribes were elated and encouraged at hearing that Caesar's forces were not invincible. The spirit of rebellion swiftly spread from one tribe to another. It soon reached Samarobriva, about three hundred miles southwest of Aduatuca, where legate Quintus Cicero was camped with his legion of no more than six thousand men. Without warning, Ambiorix's army attacked and besieged Cicero's camp. Ambiorix informed Cicero his two colleagues and their soldiers were dead. He then ordered Cicero to surrender. Cicero refused and twice sent messengers to Caesar on horseback, but they were captured and then tortured to death in plain sight of the legion. For more than a week, Ambiorix maintained his attack, but the Romans were able to fend it off.

At last, a messenger, disguised in Gallic clothing, managed to sneak through the siege line. Luckily, Caesar was still in Gaul, so it did not take long for the messenger to reach him. Cicero's letter informed Caesar that Sabinus and Cotta's legion had been annihilated, and Cicero himself was now besieged by a Gallic army. Caesar was stunned—everything he had spent years working for was beginning to unravel. Wasting no time, he immediately activated the nearest legion and marched off. He also sent messages to two other legions, instructing them to meet up with him on the march if at all possible. One legion answered the call, but the other, commanded by Labienus, wrote back saying there was another Gallic army mobilizing near his location. This was probably Caesar's first indication the revolt was bigger than only one tribe.

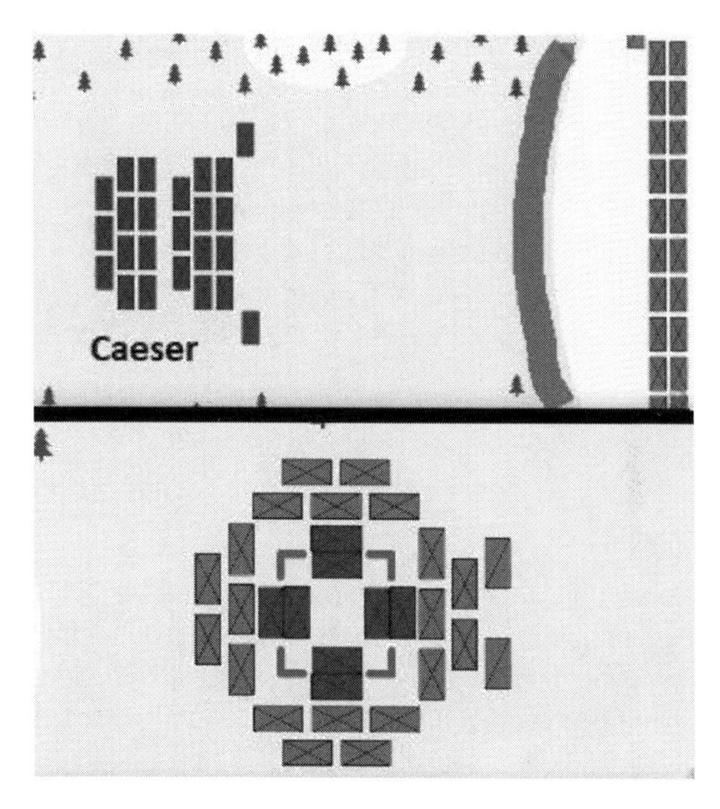

(Historia Civilis)

Caesar, in command of only two legions, marched as fast as he could to Cicero 's aid. Ambiorix's reaction was to immediately break the siege and march off to confront Caesar. When the two armies met, Caesar came upon Ambiorix positioned on a hill with a small stream running the length of his line—too strong of a defensive position for Caesar to attack. On the second day, Caesar ordered his cavalry forward, but with orders to retreat when the Gauls charged. As planned, that's exactly what happened. The Roman cavalry fell all the way back to the Roman camp, with the Gauls in hot pursuit.

When the Gauls got close, it appeared as if the Roman soldiers were in disarray. They sent word back to Ambiorix that the Romans might be on the verge of breaking, and in response, he ordered his army forward, across the stream. When the Gauls got close, they encircled the Roman camp and offered terms of surrender. The Romans responded by bursting through the gates in all four directions, taking the enemy completely by surprise. Many Gauls simply broke formation and fled, and those who held their ground were easily defeated. When news of Caesar's victory spread, the Gauls who had prevented Labienus from joining Caesar dispersed.

This revolt damaged Caesar's prestige, and he felt he needed to reassert himself. To do this, he spent the winter going from tribe to tribe demanding hostages, and attacking any tribe that had shown any disloyalty. When the snows melted, he ruthlessly attacked Ambiorix's Eburones tribe on three separate occasions, enslaving civilians and burning down villages. To bring his point home, in 53 BCE Caesar assembled all the Gallic leaders. While they looked on, he took the chief of the rebellious Senones tribe, Acco, bound him to a stake, beat him to death, and finally beheaded him.

As the second winter approached, Caesar returned to Roman territory (53-52 BCE). Everything had nearly fallen apart, but after a full year of hard work, he was finally convinced Gaul had been stabilized. But again he was wrong. The conspiracy was alive and well. The Gauls were just waiting for their moment to strike.

During the winter, the leaders of some of the largest tribes in Gaul met at a sacred grove. There they discussed Ambiorix's revolt from the previous year and the unleased attacks Caesar made on any tribe that didn't show him blind loyalty via his indiscriminate killing and enslaving of Gallic civilians.

Vercingetorix

As before, the unanimous consensus was that Caesar was laying the groundwork to conquer all of Gaul. Together, the tribal leaders agreed to formally unite against the Roman invaders. One of the individuals present at this meeting was a tribal leader named Vercingetorix. Prior to 53 BCE, Vercingetorix was employed by Julius Caesar as a mercenary cavalry commander. As a result, he gained quite a bit of insight into Roman military tactics, weapons, and warfare in general. In only a few months, Vercingetorix would rise to become the leader of a mostly united Gallic army.

With the Gallic leadership in agreement, they swore a sacred oath: *Gallic independence, or death*. Tribes of the new confederation also began to show their force and hatred for the Romans. First, a Roman trading outpost in Cenabum was stormed by the Carnute Gauls, and its inhabitants were massacred. Second, learning of the Carnutes' bold actions, other neighboring tribes followed their lead and rebelled. Third, a number of small Gallic tribes with ties to Caesar suddenly came under attack.

Caesar's right-hand man, Labienus, was put in charge of the legions while Caesar was south for the winter. When reports of these attacks reached Labienus, he kept the Roman soldiers in winter quarters, and instead sent Rome's strongest Gallic ally to deal with the problem. While these warriors dutifully marched off, after a few days they turned around and came back home, claiming the countryside was too dangerous. It was a telling sign that even one of Rome's strongest Gallic ally was suddenly unwilling to take up arms against their fellow Gauls.

Back in Roman territory, Caesar was receiving reports the Gauls had agreed to rebel and prevent Caesar from returning to Gaul. Not only that, they agreed to march on the territory of Narbonensis and take Narbo, the largest city in Transalpine Gaul. This was a situation Caesar could not allow to proceed. Narbo was a major Roman city, and if Caesar couldn't prevent attacks like this, the entire rationale behind his intervention into Gaul would be thrown into question.

This was a cunning plan on the part of the Gauls. The Alps had a reputation for being impassable during the winter. In this case, Caesar had no choice but to clear a path through one of the passes, causing the Gauls to pull back once they heard the Roman army had made it through the Alps.

Caesar left Narbo behind and headed north where he reunited with his legions in early 52 BCE. He mobilized all ten legions and ordered two to guard their food stockpile. Remember, it was winter, and the Gauls who usually supplied the Romans were under attack or had completely turned on Caser.

Caesar took the remaining eight legions, and marched straight into central Gaul. By this time, nearly all of the internal conflict within the Gallic alliance had been resolved, and Vercingetorix had emerged as the unrivaled leader of a united Gallic army. Vercingetorix's strategy was basically the Fabian strategy. Here, the goal is for one army to deprive the other of food, supplies, and reinforcements, until they become beatable on the battlefield. So when Caesar marched into central Gaul, Vercingetorix ordered over twenty nearby towns evacuated. People were allowed to take whatever they could carry, but anything left behind was burned. Vercingetorix's opening move was to go full scorched earth.

The refugees flocked to the largest settlement in the region, the fortified oppidum of Avaricum. Caesar and his legions advanced toward the oppidum, and Vercingetorix and his united Gallic army followed close behind. Avaricum was an oppidum protected by strong, high walls, as well as marshes on three sides. The Romans built their camp on the only side of the oppidum with dry land and settled in. This is known to history as the Siege of Avaricum (52 BCE), and it was miserable. The whole thing would last twenty-seven days, and it would rain the entire time.

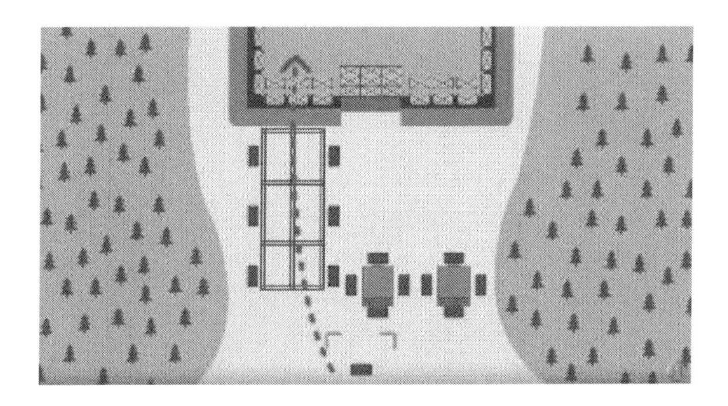

(Historia Civilis)

Caesar ordered his men to begin building two siege towers, and a gigantic wooden frame upon which the Romans could build a ramp out of earth and mud. Once completed, this ramp would allow the Romans to charge up and over the walls of Avaricum. Because of the torrential rain, construction ran into difficulties. At some point during this process, the Romans completely ran out of food. Caesar sent foraging parties out in the rain and the mud to try to find something edible for his troops.

When Vercingetorix noticed this, he moved his army closer to the Romans, and sent out Gallic patrols to deny Caesar the ability to forage. A person may wonder, if Caesar's legions were starving, why didn't he send for the food he was keeping under guard back east? If Caesar sent for it now, Vercingetorix would do everything in his power to intercept the shipment. That food had to last the Romans all year; if they lost it now, they would be forced to pull out of Gaul entirely.

When the Romans almost finished construction of their ramp, Vercingetorix asked for 10,000 volunteers from the surrounding region. He sent them around the Romans, through the marsh, into the oppidum. With the help of the volunteers, the defenders of Avaricum began improving their defenses. As the Roman ramp approached the height of the wall, the Gauls inside used wooden planks to raise their wall even higher. This back and forth extended the siege for several days.

Then, in the middle of the night, the Romans on guard duty discovered their ramp was smoldering and sinking into the ground. The Gauls dug a tunnel under their wall, and started a fire from beneath the ramp. The wooden frame was slowly starting to cave in on itself.

Without warning, the Gauls burst from the gates. They were carrying torches and buckets of tar. They started to set all of the Roman siege equipment on fire. If they could completely destroy the ramp, Caesar's attempt at taking control of Avaricum would fail. The Romans on guard duty quickly pulled the siege towers back to safety and then rushed forward to defend the ramp. The rest of the army was roused from sleep and ordered in to help. The two sides spent the rest of the night fighting for control of the ramp, with the Gauls setting fires and the Romans frantically putting them out.

When the sun rose the next day, the ramp was sinking and sagging, but still functional. The Romans spent all day repairing and raising it the last couple of feet. By the time the sun set, they were finally ready to begin the assault. The next day, the Romans took advantage of another day of heavy rainfall and fought their way up the ramp and onto the walls of

Avaricum. Apparently the Gauls were not expecting an attack in that kind of weather, but nevertheless, they rallied and fell back to a second defensive line down on the city streets within. Instead of following, the Romans stayed up on the walls, and spread out, eventually surrounding the defenders down below.

After enduring an onslaught of javelins, the Gauls resorted to the safety of their homes all the while knowing escape was no longer an option. When the Romans climbed down the walls, the legionaries roamed the streets and indiscriminately slaughtered civilians. Caesar made no attempt to stop them. When Caesar had control of the oppidum, Vercingetorix decided to pull back. He was certainly disappointed with the loss of Avaricum, but he was playing the long game and decided to wait until Caesar made his next move.

When spring arrived, Caesar was finally able to send for the two legions back east and the food they were guarding. When they arrived, Caesar divided his army into two. He gave four legions to Labienus and ordered him to march north. Caesar would take the remaining six legions and march south. Between the two armies, perhaps they could put an end to the revolt by the end of summer.

To the south, Caesar's main target was the Gallic oppidum of Gergovia. This was Vercingetorix's hometown and the capital of his tribe. As he marched south, Vercingetorix began shadowing the Roman army again, harassing it whenever he could. When Caesar reached Gergovia, he realized this might be tougher than Avaricum.

Gergovia had strong walls and was located on a giant plateau surrounded by hills. After doing some reconnaissance, Caesar realized there was aGallic garrison on top of a small hill nearby. Caesar launched a nighttime raid to capture the hill. Once he controlled the hill, he blocked a small stream which was Gergovia's only water source. Next, he dug a long defensive trench from the hill all the way back to the Roman camp.

Now, the Gauls would have to act, but to Caesar's dismay, a messenger arrived from the northeast informing Caesar there was a problem with the anticipated food shipment. The Gallic tribe that was going to deliver it apparently decided their best hope was indeed siding with Vercingetorix. Proof of this came when they began killing any Romans they could find.

After some deliberation, Caesar marched off with four legions, leaving two behind to continue the siege. By nightfall, he tracked down his rogue Gallic allies. When the Gauls saw Caesar coming, they sent a representative forward, claiming that it was all a misunderstanding. They had received some bad information and thought *Caesar* was slaughtering members of *their* tribe. Caesar had no way of knowing if he was being lied to, so he told the tribe leader that if they wanted to prove their loyalty, they would come with him and join the siege.

The next morning, Caesar's four legions returned to Gergovia with several thousand semi-treacherous Gauls and the needed food. However, when he got back to the siege, he discovered half of Vercingetorix's Gallic army was missing. When asked where they went, one of his legates said the Gauls had been systematically fortifying the surrounding hills in preparation for a flanking attack on the Roman position.

That night, Caesar sent his cavalry into the hills with orders to ride back and forth and make as much noise as possible—he wanted to confuse the Gauls. The next day, he sent his cavalry out to do the same thing, but this time was followed by one of his legions.

The Gauls saw this as an all-out attack on the hills and moved to intercept them. While they were distracted, Caesar ordered the rest of his legions forward to attack the half-strength Gallic army sitting on the plateau in front of the oppidum. The Gauls on the plateau didn't realize the Romans were attacking until they were right on top of them.

Once the Gauls on the hills realized what was really happening, they immediately turned away from the decoy cavalry and charged down the hills to attack the Romans on the plateau. When Caesar saw the Gauls coming down, he sounded the signal for a retreat. Half of his men didn't hear the signal and continued moving forward. The Gauls from the hills crashed into the oblivious Romans who took heavy losses. When the Romans realized they were out there on their own with no support, they pulled back to rejoin the rest of the army.

When news spread of Caesar's defeat at Gergovia, Rome's last Gallic ally finally sided with Vercingetorix. The Gallic cavalry which had accompanied Caesar unceremoniously rode off, and any Romans found in their territory were rounded up and killed. Gaul was now finally united in its opposition to Caesar.

Up north, Labienus had been rather successful, and had a few small victories under his belt. Caesar marched north to regroup with him and caught up somewhere near the Seine river. Together, the ten legions marched south again, probably in response to recent reports a Gallic army was marching toward Transalpine Gaul.

Changing his mind, Caesar decided to ignore these reports and focus his attention on Vercingetorix and his army. While on the march, Caesar sent ambassadors to a number of German tribes asking if they would loan him some cavalry. Because several of these tribes were interested in staying on Caesar's good side, they honored his request by sending, it is believed, several thousand horsemen.

While this was going on, Vercingetorix capitalized on his victory at Gergovia to squeeze an additional 15,000 cavalry from tribes now loyal to the cause. Vercingetorix wanted to overwhelm Caesar's column as it was marching south. With all the Gallic tribes on the look-out for Caesar, Vercingetorix soon learned of the position of the Roman army and attacked in three large groups, but the Romans responded by implementing “Roman square” formations.

Square Formation

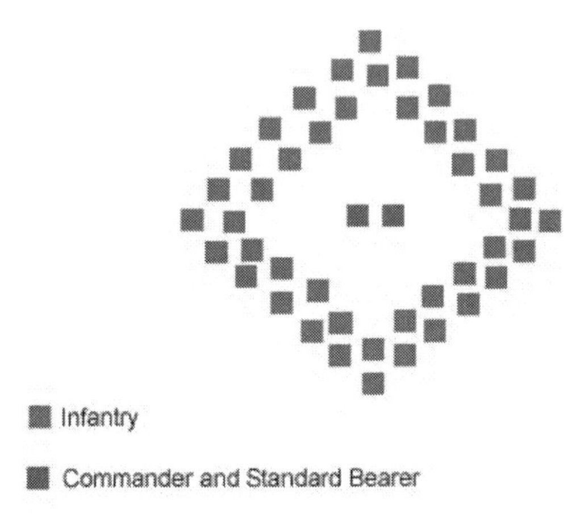

(historylink101.com)

Caesar's new German cavalry was significantly outnumbered, but they were able to use the Roman squares as protection, behind which they could launch hit-and-run attacks. Vercingetorix suffered more losses than he had expected and pulled back to the highly defensible oppidum known as Alesia. Once in position, he reasoned, first, if Caesar was foolish enough to attack the fort, he held the high ground with superior numbers and would cut him to pieces. Second, if Caesar was foolish enough to wait around, his reinforcements would arrive, and Caesar would be up against two armies instead of one.

When Caesar arrived, he quickly set to work besieging Alesia. His first stage consisted of constructing inward-facing walls that ran over ten miles, circling the Alesia, thereby cutting off any potential escape. These walls were two stories tall with raised platforms for patrols. Then, Caesar turned around and constructed another set of walls facing outwards while leaving a wide enough gap to contain his entire army. In other words, Caesar built his own fort, stealing Vercingetorix's tactical advantage out from under him. Now, if Vercingetorix wanted out, he was going to have to be the one assaulting Caesar's well-defended position. Vercingetorix's reinforcements finally arrived, and the numbers were huge. The combined Gallic armies outnumbered the Romans by 3 to 1.

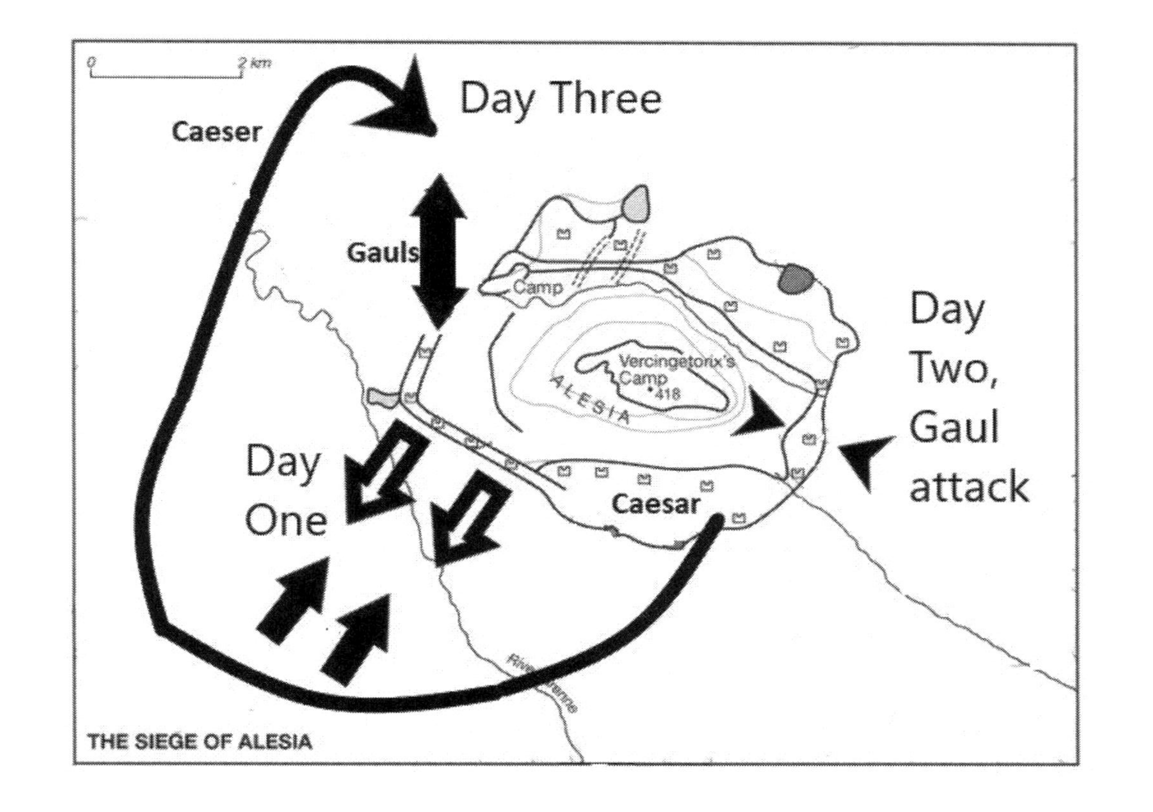
0
2 km
Caeser
Day Three
Gauls
Camp
Vercingetorix's Camp
418
ALESIA
Day Two, Gaul attack
Day One
Caesar
THE SIEGE OF ALESIA

On the very first day of the siege, the Gallic reinforcements advanced. They placed their massive cavalry in front, shielding and concealing lines of archers behind them. This set into motion an intense cavalry engagement which took place all day. Whenever the Romans thought they were gaining the upper hand, the Gallic cavalry would pull back into the range of their archers, and the Romans would retreat to escape a nasty volley of arrows.

Caesar's elite German cavalry, in a last-ditch effort, regrouped on the hillside and charged downhill, driving the Gauls into a full-fledged retreat. This time, the Romans were able to reach the Gallic archers, who were easily killed. Somehow, outnumbered and outmatched, the Romans were able to hold the Gallic cavalry off, and all sides retired for the evening.

The second day began uneventfully, but that night a focused surprise attack by the Gauls was launched from both directions (one on the interior wall and the other on the exterior wall) at one specific point in the Roman defensive line. Additional Roman troops were called over from the west sides of the Roman fort, and the Romans were barely able to hang on for the night.

On the third day, the Gauls planned for an all-out double movement assault. First they began by taking some nearby high ground outside of the enclosure that was being lightly defended by Roman infantry. Second, the Gallic relief army then launched an offensive attack along the entire Roman defensive line. The thrust of the attack was led by Vercingetorix's cousin, Vercassivellaunus, who took his men up the newly liberated hill and charged down it, attacking a weak point in the outer Roman wall. Trying to defend the entire length of the wall, Caesar took personal command and sent small groups to reinforce sections of the wall just as they were about to fall to the enemy.

Finally, Vercingetorix realized what was happening, and threw every man he had at one point along the thin interior Roman line, attempting to break through. Again when Caesar saw what was happening, he ordered every man he had in reserve to that section of the wall. Caesar was now fully committed, but Vercingetorix's breakout was prevented.

The besieged Gauls now shifted their tactics and began to attack *the entire length* of the inside wall. Caesar's army was now surrounded, fighting in all directions at once. The Roman inside wall was beginning to crumble. Vercassivellaunus, attacking downhill, at last breached the Roman western wall, and Gauls began pouring into the Roman fort. Again, Caesar, enlisting any unit he thought could be spared, threw them towards the breach in the wall. Caesar then took personal command of his cavalry and punched through the Gallic attackers at another section of the wall. The Roman cavalry then turned and charged up behind the Gauls who were pouring into Caesar's camp. The Gauls who saw the Roman cavalry charge panicked, not realizing the Romans were stretched to capacity, and this was the last card Caesar had to play.

Many Gauls tried to flee, but the Roman cavalry encircled them and either took them as prisoners or killed them outright. This allowed the Roman infantry to focus on Vercingetorix who retreated into his oppidum fort. Seeing no way out, and hoping to spare the lives of his soldiers, he dressed in beautiful ceremonial armor and rode out of the oppidum. He then circled the Roman camp on horseback, dismounted, and stripped off his armor. The Romans came forward and took him prisoner, and after six years he was executed by strangulation in his prison as according to ancient Roman custom.

The fall of Alesia did not mark the end of the Gallic Wars, but it was the final major conflict. On December 31, 52 BC, Caesar led the first of a series of punitive expeditions against other tribes involved in the rebellion. These lasted for much of the next year and culminated in the siege and capture of the town of Uxellodunum. The warriors who surrendered there had their hands cut off. They were then released as visible reminders of the price of opposing Rome. Although defeated, Vercingetorix's fame grew, and he became a popular cult figure and legend shortly after his death. The scholar Philip Matyszak notes that "the Gauls never forgot the time when they had united as a nation" and how "today he is widely recognized as the first national hero of France." The courage and resolve of Vercingetorix as he risked his life and the lives of his people to resist foreign conquest still inspires people in the modern day, and his name continues to be honored among the great heroes of the ancient world.

Conclusion

The Gauls were initially slow to adapt Roman ways until 27 CE. Under Augustus, first emperor of the Roman Empire, Romanization became rapid—at least among the ruling class. There had always been a tendency to imitate select styles and manners emanating, first, from the Mediterranean and, later, from Rome.

Once conquered, and Celtic traditional ways of gaining and expressing wealth and power (raiding and military display) were removed, it was natural for the aristocrats to adopt Roman status symbols. With Roman encouragement, fine architecture replaced weapons and gold jewelry, and feasting was displaced by Roman entertainment.

The fierce competition within and between aristocrats to outshine their rivals developed into liberal generosity in the form of building of theaters, temples, and baths which contributed to the grandeur of rustic cities. The elites also welcomed a new cultural mantle: Roman citizenship, classical learning, art, and access to a wider imperial world.

Romanization was undoubtedly helped due to the fact most urban regions were already being governed by elected magistrates. Thus, it was relatively easy to relabel existing "tribal councils" to new "city councils." The change was, thereby, made appealing by granting council members Roman citizenship with its status, tax exemptions, and further political opportunities. Consequently, Roman Gaul was governed largely by Gauls who quickly embraced the Latin language all the while carrying out their new Roman responsibilities.

Perhaps the most difficult aspect for Celtic aristocrats and warriors was to adjust to the removal of the right to bear arms and raids as ways to gain prestige. Luckily, restless spirits were able to pursue adventure and fortune in the wars of Augustus. And by the time they were discharged, Gallic recruits would have become thoroughly accustomed to Roman ways and the Latin language. Also, mercenary service was a time-honored Celtic tradition, so serving the emperor for pay was not an affront to Gallic honor.

In spite of enjoying a relatively advanced culture, and possessing a marked degree of inventive and imaginative talent in their society, nothing suggests they were able to critically evaluate the 'individual as warrior' outlet for heroic ambition and status.

This, logically, was due to the fact the Gauls never used writing for recording the historical experience of the tribe. Consequently, their knowledge remained ceremonial rather than critical. Compounding this problem, as Caesar wrote, "Their long years of wandering had not developed in them a feeling of national unity as in a love of the soil as Rome includes under the term patriotism." This then made it impossible for their tribal society to embrace a cohesive political force to resist the powerful Roman Empire.

For several centuries, Gaul remained Roman until the Western Roman Empire disintegrated into small-scale agrarian settlements as the Franks invaded in the fifth century CE. Territorial consolidation occurred in the eighth century under the Frankish King Charlemagne, who took the title of Holy Roman Emperor. After his death, his three grandsons divided his empire among themselves and held territories corresponding roughly to France, Germany, and Italy.

Appendix One:

Things recommended to view

YouTube Videos

Top 10 FASCINATING Facts About the CELTS
10. They Probably Didn't Originate in Ireland
9. The Romans Had Nothing On Their Roads
8. They Were Among the First to Utilize Iron Weaponry
7. The Celts Were Hugely Wealthy
6. They Had Slavery... Kind Of
5. They Had Progressive Views on Gender and Sexuality
4. They Weren't Savages But They Did Hunt Heads
3. The Number Three Had a Huge Significance
2. For Most of Their Existence They Were Polytheistic
1. The Celts Weren't Really, Well, "Celts"

Top 10 Surprising INNOVATIONS by the CELTS
10. Soap
9. Chainmail
8. The Horseshoe
7. Halloween
6. The Iron Plow
5. Druidism
4. Torcs
3. Coligny Calendar
2. Beltane
1. Weird Myths

Top 10 Amazing Celtic Treasures
10. Paillart Plaque
9. Witham Shield
8. Cockerel Brooch
7. Ornamental Spear Head
6. Pony Armor

5. Cultwagon Of Strettweg
4. Hochdorf Shoes
3. The Broighter Boat
2. Schwarzenbach Bowl
1. Reinheim Flagon

<u>10 Incredible Facts About the Celtic Warriors</u>
10. An Enduring (and Complicated) Legacy
9. Head Hunting
8. Style Matters
7. Hot Wheels
6. Weapons of Mass Production
5. Fashion First
4. Greetings from Rome
3. Queen Boudica
2. Vercingetorix
1. Heroes for Hire

<u>10 Fascinating Facts About the Gallic Wars</u>
10. Biased Sources
9. Julius Caesar's Backstory
8. The Populist Appeal for the Gallic Wars
7. Who were the Gauls?
6. Casus Belli
5. Ariovistus – The Germanic War Chief
4. The Bravest of the Gauls
3. The Veneti and Sea Warfare
2. Caesar in Britain
1. Vercingetorix

***

(18) *Lost Treasures Of The Ancient World* - The Celts (This is a very good overview)

The Celts - BBC Series 6 episodes)

The Celts Blood Iron And Sacrifice With Alice Roberts And Neil Oliver Episode 1 of 3. Free on Amazon Prime)

The Celts (2006 Documentary): (2 episodes. Free on Amazon Prime)

Barry Cunliffe: Who Were the Celts?

Indo-Europeans in Northern Europe part 1 (A good overview, how the Celts came about, and Celtic society.)

Indo-Europeans in Northern Europe part 2

Druids 2001 Best Movie 2016 Oscar Winner

The Gauls: Ancient Culture Analysis

Where did Celts come from? Who were the Druids? (The Introduction is a bit odd, just move to the actual film)

The Spread of the Indo-Europeans

Amazon.com

Rethinking the Gauls: Free on Amazon Prime

*   *   *

Internet

Ancient Celtic Warriors: 10 Things You Should Know
www.realmofhistory.com/2016/10/18/10-facts-ancient-celts-warriors/

Brutal and Intriguing Facts About Celtic Life
https://historycollection.co/brutal-and-intriguing-facts-about-celtic-life/

Interactive Map of the Roman Empire and Celtic Lands
http://resourcesforhistory.com/map.htm#gsc.tab=0

Appendix Two

"La Tène Era 'Celtic' Burials from France"

Irish Archaeology; Permission pending.

A number of spectacular La Tène era 'Celtic' burials have recently been uncovered by archaeologists working at Buchères in north central France. Dating from the third and fourth century BCE, these richly furnished Gaulish graves were discovered during topsoil stripping at the Aube Logistick Park.

(Wikipedia)

Of the 14 tombs excavated so far, archaeologists have unearthed five warrior burials. These men were armed with swords and spears, with two of the graves also containing evidence for shields. Originally made from leather and wood, the shields had decayed with only the orles (the metal lining perimeter) and the spina cover (the backbone) surviving.

Female burials were also identified and these had been interred with beautiful jewelry, including necklaces, fibulae and bracelets of bronze. In addition, both men and women wore large brooches on their chests, which were made from either iron or bronze, with some also decorated in coral.

These exceptional Gaulish graves are a rare discovery in this part of France and as the images below show (web site), they represent a truly remarkable find.

□

http://irisharchaeology.ie/2013/04/celtic-la-tene-era-burials-from-france/#comment-264841

"Archaeologists Uncover Royal Celtic Burial Site in Small French Town, 2015"

Archaeologists uncovered the tomb dating from the fifth century BCE in an industrial zone in the small town of Lavau, in France's Champagne region. France's National Archaeological Research Institute (Inrap), which routinely scours construction sites in order to find and preserve the country's archaeological heritage, began excavating at Lavau site in October 2014.

(Wikipedia)

The remains of an ancient Celtic prince or princess found still wearing a solid gold torque and lavish bracelets in a grave filled with riches has left archaeologists baffled.

The 2,500-year-old royal grave, which is thought to date to the fifth century BCE, was discovered in Lavau, near Troyes, is thought to have belonged to a member of a Celtic royal family.

Lying at the center of the tomb, the skeleton had been laid to rest inside an ornate two-wheeled chariot with a 1.2 lbs golden torc decorated with elaborate winged monsters around its neck. Two gold bracelets were also still on the skeleton's wrists and an armband made of jet around the left bicep.

The most exciting find has been a large bronze-decorated cauldron that was used to store watered-down wine. Inrap said it appears to have been made by Etruscan craftsmen in what is now northern Italy.

Buried inside the cauldron was a surprisingly-well preserved ceramic wine pitcher made by Greeks. The pieces are evidence of the exchanges that happened between the Mediterranean and the Celts.

Archaeologists have described the latest tomb as an 'exceptional discovery' that resembled another found in Reinheim in Germany.

Bastien Dubuis, chief archaeologist on the dig, said: 'The presence of a chariot, a cauldron and bronze crockery are three typical characteristics of a princely tomb from this period.

'They're well-documented funerary objects, objects of prestige. They were used in religious ceremonies and as a way to show off the power of the elite.'

Mediterranean merchants, seeking slaves, metals and other precious goods, opened trading channels with continental Celts, and often presented ornate goods as a kind of diplomatic gifts to local leaders.

□

Good sites:

www.thelocal.fr/20150305/fifth-century-tomb-of-celtic-prince-unearthed-in-france

The following has so wonderful photographs:

www.france24.com/en/20150305-france-archaeology-royal-celtic-prince-burial-site-lavau

"The Oppidum of Bibracte, Mont Beuvray"

Bitracte is the name of the ancient capital of the Aedui, a powerful Gallic tribe that occupied a vast territory in the heart of Burgundy, in the first century BCE. Abandoned shortly after the Roman conquest, the site of the Gallic oppidum occupies one of the highest hills of the Morvan, Mont Beuvray.

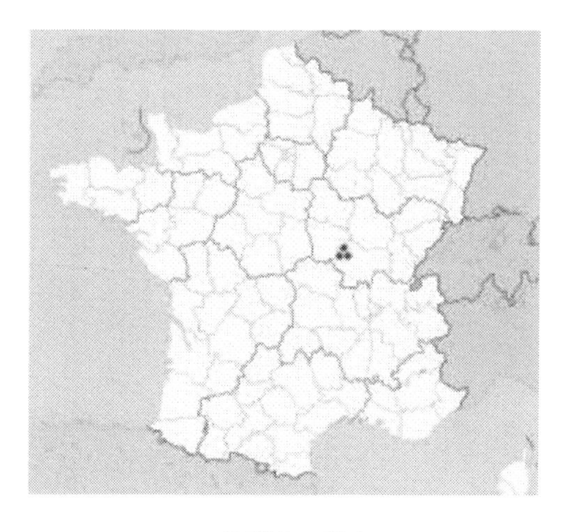

(Wikipedia)

Bibracte was rediscovered and excavated extensively in the second half of the nineteenth century. It has become a key reference site for the archaeology of the European Iron Age. Bibracte is also an emblematic historic site, where several major episodes of the Gallic Wars took place: the first decisive battle of the war, in 58 BCE; and second, the proclamation of Vercingetorix as head of the allied army against Caesar in the summer of 52 BCE.

The most striking feature about Bibracte is the contrast between wood and earth architecture in the Gaulish tradition and Mediterranean-style stone architecture which appeared shortly after the conquest of Gaul by Caesar.

Bibracte was also a busy economic center where traded goods were consumed and exchanged – principally large quantities of Italian wine and a range of items made by the town's many craftsmen.

The town of Bibracte, which lay abandoned for two millennia, is being brought back to life by the archaeologists and communities who are working to make it a site where a forgotten chapter of European history can be rediscovered.

□

Official website:

YOU will need to go the top left of the page, click on "browse" and change language to English.

www.bibracte.fr

Booklet:

https://8ce48ba6-2bdb-4079-94b3-dc3427648b00.filesusr.com/ugd/8af791_933d623964e840da8f3773d35e191f98.pdf

A movie that in part deals with Bibracte is free from Amazon Prime Video:

Rethinking the Gauls (2018)

"The Village of Vix"

Herodotus, the Greek historian, tells of a bronze jar, or krater, so big that it could hold 300 amphorae jugs of wine, the equivalent of nearly 300 gallons.

An amphorae jug

Such a krater, he says, was made by the bronze smiths of Sparta for the fabulously rich King Croesus of Lydia, who reigned from 56O to 546 BCE, about a century before Herodotus was writing.

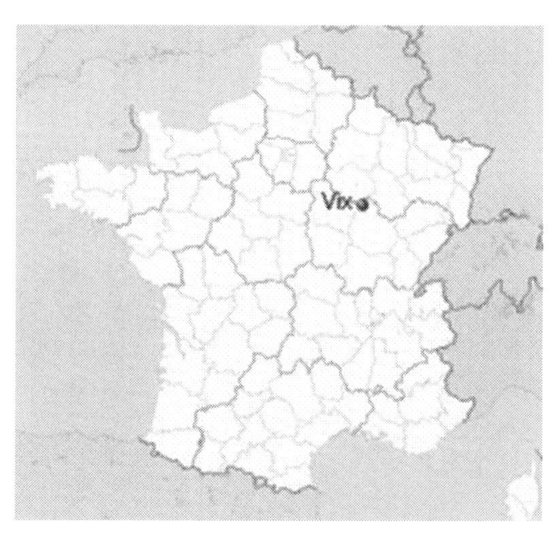

(Wikipedia)

For years, modern students of Greek history laughed off the tale of the huge vessel as a typical piece of Herodotean exaggeration. Then on one cold January morning in 1953, near the village of Vix in the Burgundy region of France, Rene Joffroy, a local archeologist, discovered the Krater of Vix, the largest known vessel from the ancient world, and one that corresponds exactly in size, age and magnificence to the jar Herodotus described.

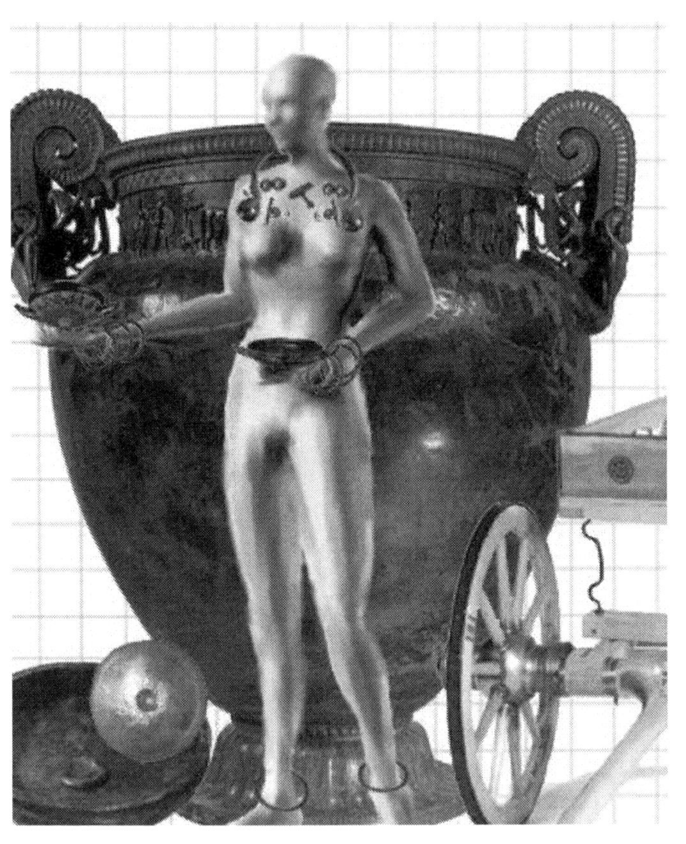

Actual size of the Lady Vix standing in front of the krater which could hold 300 gallons of wine.

The area around the village of Vix is the site of an important prehistoric complex from the Celtic Late Hallstatt and Early La Tène periods, comprising an important fortified settlement and several burial mounds. The most famous of the latter, the Vix Grave, also known as the grave of the Lady of Vix, dates to circa 500 BCE. Her grave had never been looted and contained remarkably rich grave offerings, including a great deal of jewelry and the Vix krater.

The wealth of this Celtic tribe was derived from farming (with the iron plough) from collecting tolls at the point on the Seine where the river became navigable for transport. They also exchanged tin and copper, salt, furs, and Baltic amber for luxury goods such as fine bronze objects, Greek ceramics, and coral. The cargos were shipped via the Rhone River, south to Massilia (Marseilles), to finally reach other Mediterranean ports.

In 2006, a remarkable architectural unit was discovered at the center of the site. It is a large complex of two or three buildings, the main one measuring 35 by 21 m, with an estimated height of 12 m: the dimensions of a modern church. The large hall had an apse at the back and a front porch in antis. Overall, the central unit resembles the megaron complex of early Greek architecture. Such a find is unprecedented in early Celtic Europe. The structure has been described as the "Palace" of the Lady of Vix.

"Heads of the Celtic Iron Age in the South of France" 2018

Ancient writings often describe how Celts in the Iron Age would remove the heads of their enemies to keep as trophies.

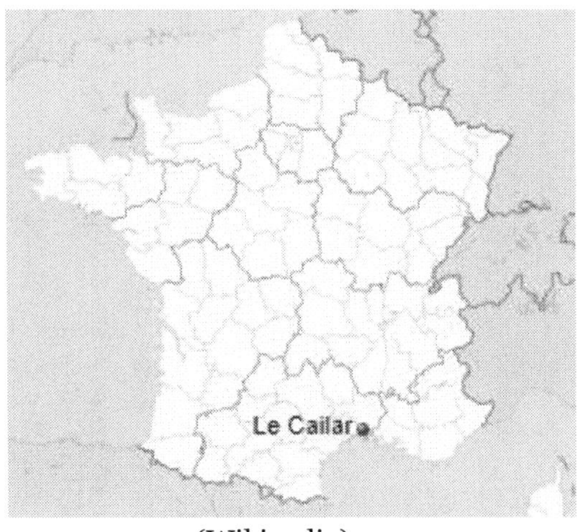

(Wikipedia)

Well over 100 fragmented human skulls were found buried in an open area of Le Cailar, France– a 2,500 year–old town on the Rhone River. The skulls, which were discovered among ancient weapons in the walled village, date back to the 3rd century B.C., when Le Cailar was a Celtic settlement.

Archaeologists recently tested 11 skulls that showed signs they had been decapitated, and had their brains removed. In some cases, tongues had also been removed.

They note also that all of the skull fragments were found inside the walls of the compound, suggesting that the heads had been mounted for those living inside, rather than as a means of frightening would-be attackers.

Though the Gauls lived for centuries in much of Europe, most of what we know about them comes from their enemies, the Romans, who considered the Gauls living on the borders of their empire as savage antagonists. In 391 B.C., during the time of the Roman Republic, the Gauls sacked the city, creating a general hatred for the Celts that lasted for centuries. That's one reason Julius Caesar's campaign to subjugate the Gauls, which began in 58 B.C., was so popular. While Caesar's war, which was ultimately successful, was supported by the people, many in the Roman Senate decried his brutal tactics and seeming lust for power, with some even suggesting he should be handed over to the enemy. This new research suggests that had those threats materialized, the Gauls would have received him in earnest, taking great care to preserve that very important balding head.

Oppida Located in France

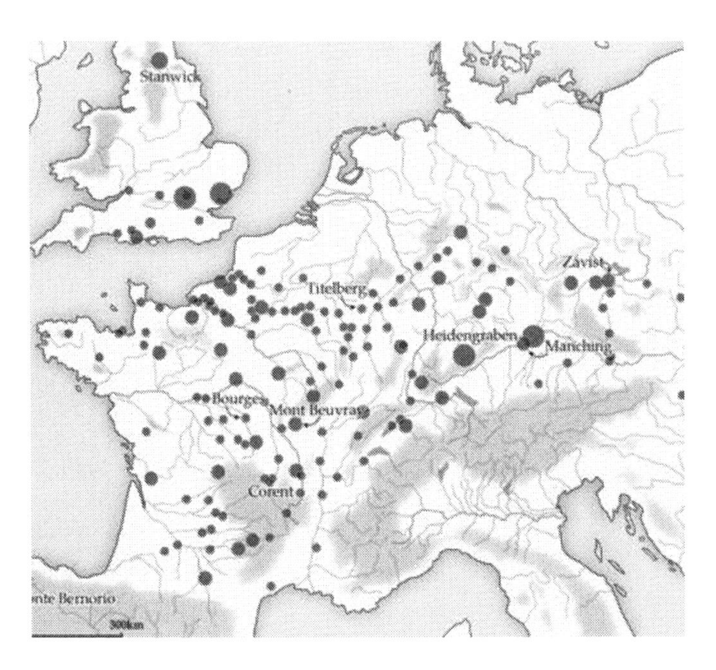

(Fernández-Götz, 2018)

Sources

Celtic Warrior: 300 BC–AD 100
Allen, Stephen

The Conquest of Gaul (Penguin Classics)
Caesar, Jane P. Gardner (Editor, Introduction), S. A. Handford (Translator)

Celts: A Captivating Guide to Ancient Celtic History and Mythology, Including Their Battles Against the Roman Republic in the Gallic Wars
Captivating History

The Ancient Celts
Cunliffe, Barry

Celts: The History and Legacy of One of the Oldest Cultures in Europe
Dougherty, Martin J.

Who Were The Celts?: Everything You Ever Wanted to Know About the Celts 1000 B.C. to the Present
Duffy, Kevin

A Brief History of the Celts
Ellis, Peter Berresford

The Celtic Empire: The First Millennium of Celtic History : C. 1000 Bc-51 Ad
Ellis, Peter Berresford

The Celts : First Masters of Europe
Eluere, Christiane

The History of Gaul: Celtic, Roman and Frankish Rule
Funck-Brentano, Frantz

The Celtic World
Green, Miranda, ED
___Green, Miranda
___Champion, Timothy
___J.N.G. & W.F

The World's Greatest Civilizations: The History and Culture of the Celts
Jesse Harasta, Charles River Editors

Atlas of the Celtic World
Haywood, John

The Celts: The People Who Came Out of the Darkness
Herm, Gerhard

The Celts of Northern Europe
Hinds, Kathryn

James, Simon

___*Exploring the World of the Celts*

___"Warriors, war, and weapons; or arms, the armed, and armed violence" The Oxford Handbook of the European Iron Age

Lost Civilizations - The Celts
Lassieur, Allison

Art of The Celts
Laing, Lloyd and Jennifer
This is online and worth looking at:
https://archive.org/details/ArtOfTheCelts/mode/1up

The Celts (This book was written to accompany a BBC series *The Celts: Blood, Iron and Sacrifice.)*
Roberts, Alice

The Pagan Celts
Ross, Anne

The Gauls: Celtic antiquities from France
Stead, I. M.

Web pages

www.visual-arts-cork.com/cultural-history-of-ireland/celtic-culture.htm
Celtic Culture (c.1,000 BCE onwards)

https://brewminate.com/celtic-warfare-from-the-ancient-hallstatt-to-la-tene-cultures/
Celtic Warfare, from the Ancient Hallstatt to La Tene Cultures

http://penelope.uchicago.edu/Thayer/E/HELP/Indexes/books.html
Works from Antiquity (index)

www.perseus.tufts.edu/hopper/text?doc=Perseus%3Atext%3A1999.04.0017%3Atext%3Dintro%3Achapter%3D1%3Asection%3D3
J. B. Greenough, Benjamin L. D'Ooge, M. Grant Daniell, Commentary on Caesar's Gallic War

https://ancientstudies.weebly.com/
Red link—*Celtic Iron Age*

www.gnrtr.com/Generator.html?pi=208&cp=3
History of Gallic Reaper

www.penn.museum/sites/expedition/the-celts-and-urbanization/
The Celts and Urbanization, The Enduring Puzzle of the Oppida

www.refitproject.com/bibracte
Resituating Europe's First Towns

http://exploringcelticciv.web.unc.edu/chapters-and-texts/
Exploring Celtic Civilizations

https://brewminate.com/an-introduction-to-the-historical-background-and-religious-customs-of-the-celts/
An Introduction to the Historical Background and Religious Customs of the Celts

www.archaeology.ru/Download/Harding/Harding_2007_The_Archaeology.pdf
Entire book: THE ARCHAEOLOGY OF CELTIC ART, D. W. Harding

Encyclopedia.com
Celts. VIX

https://unesdoc.unesco.org/ark:/48223/pf0000049777/PDF/074849engo.pdf.multi.nameddest=49777
The Unesco Courier—issue on the Celts.

www.chess.com/clubs/forum/view/what-we-dont-know-about-the-ancient-celts
What We Don't Know About the Ancient Celts

www.rando-saleve.net/pdf/celtitourpetsalev1.pdf
Who are Celtic people?

www.ancient.eu/celt/
The Celts. The Gauls. Vercingetorix

www.davidkfaux.org/LaTene_Celt_R1b1c10_part2.pdf
A Genetic Signal of Central European Celtic Ancestry: Preliminary Research Concerning Y-Chromosomal Marker S28 (Part 2)

https://brewminate.com/celtic-warfare-from-the-ancient-hallstatt-to-la-tene-cultures/
Celtic Warfare, from the Ancient Hallstatt to La Tene Cultures

www.jstor.org/stable/20513105?read_now=1&seq=
1#page_scan_tab_contents
Some Aspects of Life in Pre-Roman Gaul.

www.smithsonianmag.com/smart-news/its-true-ancient-gauls-
embalmed-severed-heads-their-enemies-180970762/
It's True: Ancient Gauls Embalmed the Severed Heads of Their Enemies

http://historyworld.net/wrldhis/PlainTextHistoriesResponsive.asp?Paragr
aphID=ddn#
HISTORY OF FRANCE

www.warhistoryonline.com/ancient-history/real-asterix-the-colorful.html
The Real Asterix: The Colorful Truth About Ancient Gaulish Warfare

www.historyfiles.co.uk/KingListsEurope/BarbarianCelts.htm
European Kingdoms: Celtic Tribes

www.penn.museum/sites/expedition/the-arrival-of-the-celts-in-ireland/
The Arrival of the Celts in Ireland

www.flickr.com/photos/28433765@N07/3220513384
Celtic god Teutates with trumpet known as the carnyx

https://www.cambridge.org/core/journals/antiquaries-
journal/article/finds-from-la-tene-in-the-british-museum-la-tene-un-site-
un-mythe-6/4AE2FDF6B405BCB413B739AD360DC402/core-reader
THE FINDS FROM LA TÈNE IN THE BRITISH MUSEUM

https://periklisdeligiannis.wordpress.com/2019/01/23/fortress-of-paule-
armorica-gaul-50-bce/#more-8202
Fortress of Paule, Armorica, Gaul 50 BCE

https://realmsofgoldthenovel.blogspot.com/2012/07/the-vix-burial.html
The Vix Krater and the Lady of Vix Was she Princess, Priestess, Queen?

www.livingmyths.com/Celticyear.htm
The Celtic Year

www.sacredfire.net/festivals.html
The Fire Festivals

YouTube

Historia Civilis:

(Some maps came from these pages. I am also a Patreon member of HC.)

Caesar in Gaul: Makin' Waves (56 B.C.E.)

Caesar in Gaul: REVOLT! (54 to 53 B.C.E.)

The Battle of Alesia (52 B.C.E.)

Vercingetorix (52 to 50 B.C.E.)

Other books in this series:

The 'I Wish I Knew That Before Visiting France' Guidebook

A Short History of France for Teens and Exchange Students

Charlemagne: Volume 1: Carolingian Dynasty Rise to Power and the Saxon war

Eleanor of Aquitaine: A Short Biography

The French Resistance: A Brief Introduction

The Life of Josephine Baker and Her 2021 Induction into France's Pantheon

David B. McCoy earned his history teaching degree from Ashland University and his graduate degree from Kent State University. After teaching thirty-two years, David retired to write short books on a wide variety of topics.

Short, concise, and informative, most Spare Change Press ® publications are generally less than 100 pages.

www.amazon.com/author/davidmcco

Made in United States
Orlando, FL
07 September 2023